Collins

# Unlocking
# JAPANESE
## with
# Paul Noble

Published by Collins
An imprint of HarperCollins Publishers
Westerhill Road
Bishopbriggs
Glasgow G64 2QT

HarperCollinsPublishers
1st Floor, Watermarque Building
Ringsend Road, Dublin 4, Ireland

First edition 2022

10 9 8 7 6 5 4 3 2 1

© Paul Noble 2022

ISBN 978-0-00-842187-8
ISBN 978-0-00-854717-2

Typeset by Davidson Publishing Solutions,
Glasgow

Printed in Italy by Grafica Veneta S.p.A.

If you would like to comment on any aspect
of this book, please contact us at the given
address or online.
E-mail dictionaries@harpercollins.co.uk
www.facebook.com/collinsdictionary
@CollinsDict

**Acknowledgements**
Images from Shutterstock.

MANAGING EDITOR
Maree Airlie

CONTRIBUTORS
Harumi Currie
Alice Grandison
Kate Mohideen

FOR THE PUBLISHER
Gerry Breslin
Gordon MacGilp
Lauren Murray

**People who know no Japanese at all.**

People who know some Japanese already.

People learning Japanese for the first time.

People coming back to the language after a break.

People who didn't like how languages were taught at school.

People who are amazed by just how closely grammar books resemble furniture assembly instructions.

# Who is this book for?

*People who think they can't learn a foreign language.*

People who've listened to one of Paul Noble's audio courses.

People who haven't listened to one of Paul Noble's audio courses.

People who have studied Japanese before.

People who haven't studied Japanese before.

People curious about whether they can learn a language.

**People who feel confused by the way languages are normally taught.**

# Contents

Did you know you
already speak Japanese?

# Did you know you already speak Japanese?

Did you know you already speak Japanese? That you hear it in the street? That you've used it with your friends, with your family, at work, in the supermarket?

**Were you aware of that fact?**

**Well, even if you weren't, it's nevertheless true.**

Of course, you might not have realised at the time that what you were reading / saying / hearing was actually Japanese but I can prove to you that it was. Just take a look at these words below:

| | | | |
|---|---|---|---|
| emoji | futon | tycoon | karaoke |
| origami | manga | satsuma | sushi |
| tofu | zen | karate | ninja | tsunami |

Have you read through them?
yes? Good.

Now, answer me this, are they:

A: English words
B: Japanese words
C: Both

Well, if you're reading this book then you're clearly already a highly intelligent person with good judgement, so you will have correctly chosen "C".

Yes, these are words that we have in English *but* they do of course originate from Japanese. And these are by no means isolated examples of words that are shared by both English and Japanese; rather they are merely the tip of a by no means tiny iceberg.

This is because not only are there many Japanese words that have come into English over the centuries but there are also *even more* English words that have gone into Japanese.

If we begin by using these words, together with an extremely subtle method that shows you how to put them into sentences in a way that's almost effortless, then becoming competent at speaking Japanese becomes far, far easier.

The only thing that *you* will need to do to make this happen is to follow the three simple rules printed on the following pages. These rules will explain to you how to use this book so that you can begin unlocking the Japanese language for yourself in a matter of hours.

well, what are you waiting for?
Turn the page!

# Rule Number 1:

# Don't skip anything!

Using this book is extremely simple – and highly effective – *if* you follow its three simple rules.

If you don't want to follow them then I recommend that, instead of reading the book, you use it to prop up a wobbly coffee table, as it won't work if you don't follow the rules. Now get ready – because here's the first one!

Each and every little thing in this book has been put where it is, in a very particular order, for a very particular reason. So, if the book asks you to read or do something, then do it! Who's the teacher after all, you or me, eh? Also, each part of the book builds on and reinforces what came before it. So, if you start skipping sections, you will end up confused and lost! Instead, you should just take your time and gently work your way through the book at your own pace – *but without skipping anything*!

Step
by
Step

# Rule Number 2:

# Don't try to memorise anything!

Trying to jam things into your head is boring *and* it doesn't work. People often cram for tests and then forget everything the moment they walk out of the exam. Clearly, we don't want that happening here.

Instead, I have designed this book so that any word or idea taught in it will come up multiple times. So, you don't need to worry about trying to remember or memorise anything because the necessary repetition is actually already built-in. In fact, trying to memorise what you're learning is likely to hinder rather than help your progress.

So, just work your way through the book in a relaxed way and, if you happen to forget something, don't worry because, as I say, you will be reminded of it again, multiples times, later on.

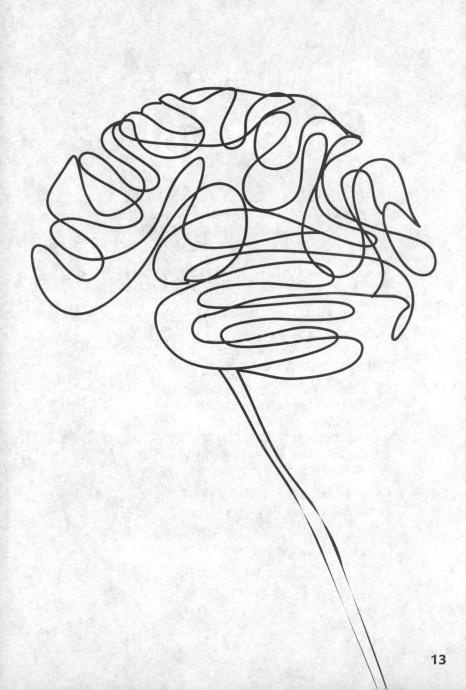

# Rule Number 3:
# Cover up!

No, I'm not being a puritan grandmother and telling you to put on a long-sleeved cardigan. Instead, I'm asking you to take a bookmark or piece of paper and use it to cover up any **red text** that you come across as you work your way through the book.

These **red bits** are the answers to the various riddles, challenges, and questions that I will pose as I lead you into the Japanese language. If you read these answers without at least trying to work out the solutions to the various riddles and challenges first, then the book simply won't work for you!

So, make sure to use something to cover up the bits of **red text** in the book while you have a go at trying to work out the answers – it doesn't matter if you sometimes get them wrong because it is by trying to think out the answers that you will learn how to use the language.

Trust me on this, you will see that it works from the very first page!

Take a look at the page on the right to see how to use your bookmark or piece of paper to cover up correctly.

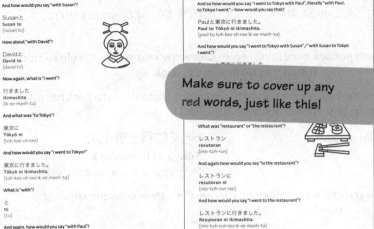

And how would you say "with Susan"?

Susanと
**Susan to**
(susan to)

How about "with David"?

Davidと
**David to**
(david to)

Now again, what is "I went"?

行きました
**ikimashita**
(k-ee-mash-ta)

And what was "to Tokyo"?

東京に
**Tōkyō ni**
(toh-kee-oh nee)

And how would you say "I went to Tokyo"?

東京に行きました。
**Tōkyō ni ikimashita.**
(toh-kee-oh nee k-ee-mash-ta)

What is "with"?

と
**to**
(to)

And again, how would you say "with Paul"?

Paulと
**Paul to**
(paul to)

22

And so how would you say "I went to Tokyo with Paul", literally "with Paul, to Tokyo I went" – how would you say that?

Paulと東京に行きました。
**Paul to Tōkyō ni ikimashita.**
(paul to toh-kee-oh nee ik-ee-mash-ta)

And how would you say "I went to Tokyo with Susan" / "with Susan to Tokyo I went"?

Make sure to cover up any red words, just like this!

What was "restaurant" or "the restaurant"?

レストラン
**resutoran**
(res-toh-run)

And again how would you say "to the restaurant"?

レストランに
**resutoran ni**
(res-toh-run nee)

And how would you say "I went to the restaurant"?

レストランに行きました。
**Resutoran ni ikimashita.**
(res-toh-run nee ik-ee-mash-ta)

What is "with Paul"?

Paulと
**Paul to**
(paul to)

23

And how would you say "with Susan"?

Susanと
**Susan to**
(susan to)

How about "with David"?

Davidと
**David to**
(david to)

Now again, what is "I went"?

行きました
**ikimashita**
(k-ee-mash-ta)

And what was "to Tokyo"?

東京に
**Tōkyō ni**
(toh-kee-oh nee)

And how would you say "I went to Tokyo"?

東京に行きました。
**Tōkyō ni ikimashita.**
(toh-kee-oh nee k-ee-mash-ta)

What is "with"?

と
**to**
(to)

And again, how would you say "with Paul"?

Paulと
**Paul to**
(paul to)

22

And so how would you say "I went to Tokyo with Paul", literally "with Paul, to Tokyo I went" – how would you say that?

Paulと東京に行きました。
**Paul to Tōkyō ni ikimashita.**
(paul to toh-kee-oh nee ik-ee-mash-ta)

And how would you say "I went to Tokyo with Susan" / "with Susan to Tokyo I went"?

Susanと東京に行きました。
**Susan to Tōkyō ni ikimashita.**
(susan to toh-kee-oh nee ik-ee-mash-ta)

Then, having tried to work out the answer, uncover and check!

resutoran
(res-toh-run)

And again how would you say "to the restaurant"?

レストランに
**resutoran ni**
(res-toh-run nee)

And how would you say "I went to the restaurant"?

レストランに行きました。
**Resutoran ni ikimashita.**
(res-toh-run nee ik-ee-mash-ta)

What is "with Paul"?

Paulと
**Paul to**
(paul to)

23

# Oh, and just one more thing before we begin...

There's just one more thing I need to let you know before we begin and it's to do with how I've written the Japanese in this book.

Once you begin, you'll see that each English sentence in the book has three translations of it into Japanese. For example:

I went to Tokyo.　　　　　　東京に行きました。
**Tōkyō ni ikimashita.**
(toh-kee-oh nee ik-ee-mash-ta)

Now you might be wondering, why are there three different versions? What are they for?

Well, to begin with, please be aware that all three versions say exactly the same thing in Japanese.

The top version is simply a translation of the English that has been written in Japanese script.

The middle version is a translation of the English that has been written in the official, Romanised form of Japanese, known as "rōmaji". It is used by non-Japanese to read the language.

The final, bottom version of the Japanese is my own personal pronunciation guide, which is designed to show you how to pronounce the language if you can't already read Japanese characters (a distinct possibility) and if you also sometimes feel uncertain about how exactly to pronounce the rōmaji. So, this is an extra bit of guidance, with the Japanese words spelled the way they might be if they were English words.

So, they're the three versions of Japanese you'll see throughout the book – please use whichever one(s) help you the most!

Okay now, let's begin!

# CHAPTER 1

I ate katsu curry
in that restaurant
yesterday!

# I ate katsu curry in that restaurant yesterday!

The English sentence above isn't that complicated, is it? Or is it...?

Well, I have taught many people over the years, including those who know no Japanese at all through to those who may have spent several years trying to learn the language. And yet, whether they have studied the language before or not, hardly any of them arrive in my classroom able to construct a seemingly simple sentence like this when I first meet them.

Admittedly, they might know how to say other far less useful things, like "I'm 37 years old and have two sisters" – an unusual conversation opener for an adult from my perspective – but they nevertheless are frequently unable to say what they ate the day before or where they ate it!

Well, in just a few minutes' time, you *will* be able to do this – even if you've never learnt any Japanese before.

Just remember though: ***don't* skip anything, *don't* waste your time trying to memorise anything but *do* use your bookmark to cover up anything red you find on each page.**

## Okay now, let's begin!

"Tokyo" in Japanese is:

東京
**Tōkyō**
(pronounced "toh-kee-oh")

And "to" in Japanese is:

に
**ni**
(pronounced "nee")

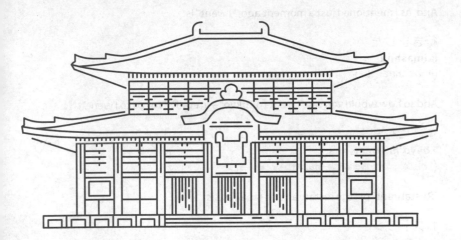

If you want to say "to Tokyo" in Japanese, you'll literally say "Tokyo to". How do you think you would say that?

東京に
**Tōkyō ni**
(toh-kee-oh nee)

> Did you remember to cover up the red words while you worked out the answer?

"I went" in Japanese is:

行きました
**ikimashita**
(ik-ee-mash-ta)

If you want to say "I went to Tokyo", you'll literally say "Tokyo to I went". Before you say that, however, remind me, what was "Tokyo"?

東京
**Tōkyō**
(toh-kee-oh)

And what was "to Tokyo"?

東京に
**Tōkyō ni**
(toh-kee-oh nee)

And, as I mentioned just a moment ago, "I went" is:

行きました
**ikimashita**
(ik-*ee*-mash-ta)

And so how would you say "I went to Tokyo" – literally "Tokyo to I went"?

東京に行きました。
**Tōkyō ni ikimashita.**
(toh-kee-oh nee ik-ee-mash-ta)

"Restaurant" or "the restaurant" in Japanese is:

レストラン
**resutoran**
(res-toh-run)

Now remind me, how do you say "to Tokyo"?

東京に
**Tōkyō ni**
(toh-kee-oh nee)

And which part of that means "to"?

に
**ni**
(nee)

And again, what was "restaurant" or "the restaurant"?

レストラン
**resutoran**
(res-toh-run)

And so how do you think you would say "to the restaurant"?

レストランに
**resutoran ni**
(res-toh-run nee)

Notice how, as with "to Tokyo" the "to" part goes *after* the place in Japanese, not before as in English.

What is "I went"?

行きました
**ikimashita**
(ik-ee-mash-ta)

And so how would you say "I went to the restaurant" – literally "to the restaurant I went"?

レストランに行きました。
**Resutoran ni ikimashita.**
(res-toh-run nee ik-ee-mash-ta)

And again, what was "I went to Tokyo"?

東京に行きました。
**Tōkyō ni ikimashita.**
(toh-kee-oh nee ik-ee-mash-ta)

"With" in Japanese is:

と
**to**
(to[1])

If you want to say "with Paul" in Japanese, you will literally say "Paul with". How would you say that?

Paulと
**Paul to**
(paul to)

---

1    As you'll have noticed, under each set of Japanese words, I have provided pronunciation guidance in brackets. If there's something that might need some additional clarification, however, I'll also add a little footnote like this one to give you some extra help. In this case, I'm going to help you with the pronunciation of "to" ("with").

The Japanese word for "with" – "to" – should be pronounced like the "to" in the English word "top". Pronounce it that way and you'll definitely be understood!

And how would you say "with Susan"?

Susanと
**Susan to**
(susan to)

How about "with David"?

Davidと
**David to**
(david to)

Now again, what is "I went"?

行きました
**ikimashita**
(ik-ee-mash-ta)

And what was "to Tokyo"?

東京に
**Tōkyō ni**
(toh-kee-oh nee)

And how would you say "I went to Tokyo"?

東京に行きました。
**Tōkyō ni ikimashita.**
(toh-kee-oh nee ik-ee-mash-ta)

What is "with"?

と
**to**
(to)

And again, how would you say "with Paul"?

Paulと
**Paul to**
(paul to)

And so how would you say "I went to Tokyo with Paul", literally "with Paul, to Tokyo I went". How would you say that?

Paulと東京に行きました。
**Paul to Tōkyō ni ikimashita.**
(paul to toh-kee-oh nee ik-ee-mash-ta)

And how would you say "I went to Tokyo with Susan" / "with Susan to Tokyo I went"?

Susanと東京に行きました。
**Susan to Tōkyō ni ikimashita.**
(susan to toh-kee-oh nee ik-ee-mash-ta)

How about "I went to Tokyo with David"?

David と東京に行きました。
**David to Tōkyō ni ikimashita.**
(david to toh-kee-oh nee ik-ee-mash-ta)

What was "restaurant" or "the restaurant"?

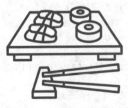

レストラン
**resutoran**
(res-toh-run)

And again how would you say "to the restaurant"?

レストランに
**resutoran ni**
(res-toh-run nee)

And how would you say "I went to the restaurant"?

レストランに行きました。
**Resutoran ni ikimashita.**
(res-toh-run nee ik-ee-mash-ta)

What is "with Paul"?

Paulと
**Paul to**
(paul to)

And so how would you say "I went to the restaurant with Paul"?

Paulとレストランに行きました。
**Paul to resutoran ni ikimashita.**
(paul to res-toh-run nee ik-ee-mash-ta)

And "I went to the restaurant with Susan"?

Susanとレストランに行きました。
**Susan to resutoran ni ikimashita.**
(susan to res-toh-run nee ik-ee-mash-ta)

"I ate" in Japanese is:

食べました
**tabemashita**
(ta-bay-mash-ta)

So how would you say "I ate with Susan" – literally "with Susan I ate"?

Susanと食べました。
**Susan to tabemashita.**
(susan to ta-bay-mash-ta)

How about "I ate with Paul"?

Paulと食べました。
**Paul to tabemashita.**
(paul to ta-bay-mash-ta)

And "I ate with David"?

Davidと食べました。
**David to tabemashita.**
(david to ta-bay-mash-ta)

"Sushi" in Japanese is, of course:

すし
**sushi**
(sushi[2])

---

2  You have hopefully noticed that I've given the pronunciation guidance for "sushi" simply as "sushi". This is because the word in Japanese is pronounced in a very similar way to how it is in English. The only difference is that both the "su" and "shi" sounds are even shorter in Japanese than they are in English. So "sushi" in Japanese sounds a bit like someone saying "sushi" in English but as if they were in a hurry to get the word out of their mouths!

Now, if you want to say "I ate sushi" in Japanese, you'll find that when you say "sushi" you'll follow it with an "o" – pronounced like the "o" in "hot" or "not".

Now you may be wondering, why on earth would I want to put an "o" after the word "sushi"? Well, you'll do this in Japanese because the "o" is there to make it clear to the person listening to you that the sushi – the thing before the "o" – is the thing that you're eating. It's like a finger pointing back at the sushi, saying "this is the thing I'm referring to, the thing that I ate." Anyway, don't worry or think about this too much, as the best way to understand it is to simply start using it. Let me show you how:

Again, what was "sushi" in Japanese?

すし
**sushi**
(sushi)

Now I want you to put an "o" after the "sushi". Do that now, say "sushi" followed by "o." What will that sound like?

すしを
**Sushi o**
(sushi o)

Now, do you remember how to say "I ate"?

食べました
**tabemashita**
(ta-bay-mash-ta)

And so now say "I ate sushi" – or more literally, as the Japanese say it, "sushi o I ate."

すしを食べました。
**Sushi o tabemashita.**
(sushi o ta-bay-mash-ta)

So, as you can see, you've put an "o" after the word "sushi" and in doing so you have made it clear to the person you're talking to that the sushi is the thing that you've eaten.

"Ramen" in Japanese is, of course:

ラーメン
**rāmen**
(ra-men)

## What is ramen exactly (if you didn't already know)?

Ramen is a type of Japanese noodle soup. It uses wheat noodles served in a broth; that broth can be salt, soy sauce, miso, pork bone or fish flavoured. It will often include ingredients such as scallions, sliced pork, seaweed or more or less anything you could imagine. Each region of Japan has its own ramen speciality – and you'll learn about some of them here. Anyway, for the moment, simply be aware that ramen = noodle soup.

So, how would you say "I ate ramen" – literally "ramen o I ate"?

ラーメンを食べました。
**Rāmen o tabemashita.**
(ra-men o ta-bay-mash-ta)

And again, how would you say "I ate sushi"?

すしを食べました。
**Sushi o tabemashita.**
(sushi o ta-bay-mash-ta)

What is "with Paul"?

Paulと
**Paul to**
(paul to)

So how would you say "I ate sushi with Paul" / "with Paul sushi I ate"?

Paulとすしを食べました。
**Paul to sushi o tabemashita.**
(paul to sushi o ta-bay-mash-ta)

How about "I ate ramen with Paul"?

Paulとラーメンを食べました。
**Paul to rāmen o tabemashita.**
(paul to ra-men o ta-bay-mash-ta)

"Mr", "Mrs", "Miss" or "Ms" in Japanese are all:

さん
**san**
(sun)

And if you wanted to say "Mr Suzuki" for instance, you'd say:

鈴木さん
**Suzuki san**
(su-zoo-kee sun)

So, literally that's "Suzuki Mr".

How do you think you'd say "Ms Tanaka"?

田中さん
**Tanaka san**
(ta-na-ka sun)

How about "Ms Suzuki"?

鈴木さん
**Suzuki san**
(su-zoo-kee sun)

How do you think you would say "*with* Ms Suzuki"?

鈴木さんと
**Suzuki san to**
(su-zoo-kee sun to)

Now again, what is "I ate ramen"?

ラーメンを食べました。
**Rāmen o tabemashita.**
(ra-men o ta-bay-mash-ta)

And so how would you say "I ate ramen with Ms Suzuki"?

鈴木さんとラーメンを食べました。
**Suzuki san to rāmen o tabemashita.**
(su-zoo-kee sun to ra-men o ta-bay-mash-ta)

And how would you say "I ate sushi with Mr Tanaka"?

田中さんとすしを食べました。
**Tanaka san to sushi o tabemashita.**
(ta-na-ka sun to sushi o ta-bay-mash-ta)

Once again, what is "restaurant"?

レストラン
**resutoran**
(res-toh-run)

And what is "I went"?

行きました
**ikimashita**
(ik-ee-mash-ta)

And how would you say "I went to the restaurant"?

レストランに行きました。
**Resutoran ni ikimashita.**
(res-toh-run nee ik-ee-mash-ta)

"Department store" or "the department store" in Japanese is:

デパート
**depāto**
(day-par-toh)

So how would you say "to the department store"?

デパートに
**depāto ni**
(day-par-toh nee)

How about "I went to the department store"?

デパートに行きました。
**Depāto ni ikimashita.**
(day-par-toh nee ik-ee-mash-ta)

And how would you say "I went to the department store with Ms Tanaka"?

田中さんとデパートに行きました。
**Tanaka san to depāto ni ikimashita.**
(ta-na-ka sun to day-par-toh nee ik-ee-mash-ta)

What about "I went to the restaurant with Miss Suzuki"?

鈴木さんとレストランに行きました。
**Suzuki san to resutoran ni ikimashita.**
(su-zoo-kee sun to res-toh-run nee ik-ee-mash-ta)

Now, just on its own again, what is "restaurant" or "the restaurant"?

レストラン
**resutoran**
(res-toh-run)

"in the restaurant" in Japanese is:

レストランで
**resutoran de**
(res-toh-run day)

Now again, what was "I ate"?

食べました
**tabemashita**
(ta-bay-mash-ta)

And what was "in the restaurant"?

レストランで
**resutoran de**
(res-toh-run day)

And so how would you say "I ate in the restaurant" – literally "in the restaurant I ate"?

レストランで食べました。
**Resutoran de tabemashita.**
(res-toh-run day ta-bay-mash-ta)

What is "sushi"?

すし
**sushi**
(sushi)

And how would you say "I ate sushi"?

すしを食べました。
**Sushi o tabemashita.**
(sushi o ta-bay-mash-ta)

Did you remember to add the "o" after the word "sushi" to make it clear that the "sushi" is the thing that's been eaten? Don't worry if you didn't, as you'll now certainly remember to add it for the next sentence.

How would you say "I ate ramen"?

ラーメンを食べました。
**Rāmen o tabemashita.**
(ra-men o ta-bay-mash-ta)

And again what is "in the restaurant"?

レストランで
**resutoran de**
(res-toh-run day)

And so how do you think you would say "I ate ramen in the restaurant"?

レストランでラーメンを食べました。
**Resutoran de rāmen o tabemashita.**
(res-toh-run day ra-men o ta-bay-mash-ta)

How about "I ate sushi in the restaurant"?

レストランですしを食べました。
**Resutoran de sushi o tabemashita.**
(res-toh run day sushi o ta-bay-mash-ta)

As I mentioned earlier, "department store" or "the department store" in Japanese is:

デパート
**depāto**
(day-par-toh)

So how would you say "*in* the department store"?

デパートで
**depāto de**
(day-par-toh day)

And how would you say "I ate sushi in the department store"?

デパートですしを食べました。
**Depāto de sushi o tabemashita.**
(day-par-toh day sushi o ta-bay-mash-ta)

How about "I ate ramen in the department store"?

デパートでラーメンを食べました。
**Depāto de ramen o tabemashita.**
(day-par-toh day ra-men o ta-bay-mash-ta)

Just a quick note about word order. You must certainly have noticed that the word order in Japanese is different than in English. And so you may well be asking yourself, "How exactly does it work? What are the rules?" Well, the most important rule in Japanese is that the thing you've done should go at the end of the sentence.

So, if the thing you did was that you *ate something*, then that should go at the end of the sentence. Let's practise doing that. What is "I ate"?

食べました
**tabemashita**
(ta-bay-mash-ta)

So that's what you did – you ate something – and so it should go at the end of the sentence. More specifically, you ate "ramen", so let's add that into the sentence. How would you say "I ate ramen"?

ラーメンを食べました。
**Rāmen o tabemashita.**
(ra-men o ta-bay-mash-ta)

So, what we've done is we've eaten ramen and we've put what we've done (eating ramen) at the end of the sentence. If we want to add anything more to the sentence, we can simply put it in front of this part. For instance, what is "in the restaurant"?

レストランで
**resutoran de**
(res-toh-run day)

So how would you say "I ate ramen in the restaurant"?

レストランでラーメンを食べました。
**Resutoran de rāmen o tabemashita.**
(res-toh-run day ra-men o ta-bay-mash-ta)

So again, the thing you did – the "I ate" part – goes at the end of the sentence and everything else goes before it.

How would you say "I ate sushi in the restaurant"?

レストランですしを食べました。
**Resutoran de sushi o tabemashita.**
(res-toh-run day sushi o ta-bay-mash-ta)

What is "with"?

と
**to**
(to)

And how would you say "with Ms Suzuki"?

鈴木さんと
**Suzuki san to**
(su-zoo-kee sun to)

And how would you say "I ate sushi with Ms Suzuki"?

鈴木さんとすしを食べました。
**Suzuki san to sushi o tabemashita.**
(su-zoo-kee sun to sushi o ta-bay-mash-ta)

How about "I ate ramen with Mr Tanaka"?

田中さんとラーメンを食べました。
**Tanaka san to rāmen o tabemashita.**
(ta-na-ka sun to ra-men o ta-bay-mash-ta)

So again, just as you saw earlier, the thing you did (the "I ate" part) goes at the end of the sentence. Everything else (for instance what you ate or who you ate it with) goes before it.

Now once more, how would you say "I ate ramen in the restaurant"?

レストランでラーメンを食べました。
**Resutoran de rāmen o tabemashita.**
(res-toh-run day ra-men o ta-bay-mash-ta)

"Katsu curry" in Japanese is:

カツカレー
**katsu karē**
(kats ka-ray)

So how would you say "I ate katsu curry"?

カツカレーを食べました。
**Katsu karē o tabemashita.**
(kats ka-ray o ta-bay-mash-ta)

How about "I ate katsu curry with Paul"?

Paulとカツカレーを食べました。
**Paul to katsu karē o tabemashita.**
(paul to kats ka-ray o ta-bay-mash-ta)

And "I ate katsu curry in the restaurant"?

## レストランでカツカレーを食べました。
**Resutoran de katsu karē o tabemashita.**
(res-toh-run kats ka-ray o ta-bay-mash-ta)

Now, if you wanted to say an even longer sentence, such as "I ate katsu curry in the restaurant with Paul", you might again wonder what the right word order would be.

Well, you already know that the thing you did – the "I ate" part – goes at the end.

For the other bits of the sentence, we'll simply say that it will sound very natural, neutral and good if you put the *with* part of the sentence before the *in* part. So, from now on, if you have a "with..." and an "in..." in a sentence, put the "with" part before the "in" part. Let's try doing that that now:

Say "I ate katsu curry in the restaurant with Paul" – or, as Japanese speakers will say it, "with Paul in the restaurant katsu curry I ate":

## Paulとレストランでカツカレーを食べました。
**Paul to resutoran de katsu karē o tabemashita.**
(paul to res-toh-run day kats ka-ray o ta-bay-mash-ta)

And how would you say "I ate katsu curry in the restaurant with Mr Suzuki" / "with Mr Suzuki in the restaurant katsu curry I ate":

## 鈴木さんとレストランでカツカレーを食べました。
**Suzuki san to resutoran de katsu karē o tabemashita.**
(su-zoo-kee sun to res-toh-run day kats ka-ray o ta-bay-mash-ta)

How about "I ate sushi in the restaurant with Ms Tanaka"?

## 田中さんとレストランですしを食べました。
**Tanaka san to resutoran de sushi o tabemashita.**
(ta-na-ka sun to res-toh-run day sushi o ta-bay-mash-ta)

What is "the department store"?

## デパート
**depāto**
(day-par-toh)

And how would you say "in the department store"?

デパートで
**depāto de**
(day-par-toh day)

What about "I ate in the department store"?

デパートで食べました。
**Depāto de tabemashita.**
(day-par-toh day ta-bay-mash-ta)

And how about "I ate katsu curry in the department store"?

デパートでカツカレーを食べました。
**Depāto de katsu karē o tabemashita.**
(day-par-toh day kats ka-ray o ta-bay-mash-ta)

And how would you say "I ate katsu curry in the department store with Paul"?

Paulとデパートでカツカレーを食べました。
**Paul to depāto de katsu karē o tabemashita.**
(paul to day-par-toh day kats ka-ray o ta-bay-mash-ta)

What about "I ate ramen in the department store with Paul"?

Paulとデパートでラーメンを食べました。
**Paul to depāto de rāmen o tabemashita.**
(paul to day-par-toh day ra-men o ta-bay-mash-ta)

"*That* department store" in Japanese would be:

あのデパート
**ano depāto**
(an-oh day-par-toh)

So how do you think you would you say "*in* that department store"?

あのデパートで
**ano depāto de**
(an-oh day-par-toh day)

And how would you say "I ate in that department store"?

あのデパートで食べました。
**Ano depāto de tabemashita.**
(an-oh day-par-toh day ta-bay-mash-ta)

How about "I ate katsu curry in that department store"?

あのデパートでカツカレーを食べました。
**Ano depāto de katsu karē o tabemashita.**
(an-oh day-par-toh day kats ka-ray o ta-bay-mash-ta)

"Yesterday" in Japanese is:

昨日
**kinō**
(kee-noh)

So how would you say "Yesterday, I ate katsu curry in that department store"?

昨日、あのデパートでカツカレーを食べました。
**Kinō, ano depāto de katsu karē o tabemashita.**
(kee-noh an-oh day-par-toh day kats ka-ray o ta-bay-mash-ta)

Now again, what is "restaurant"?

レストラン
**resutoran**
(res-toh-run)

And so how do you think you would say "*that* restaurant"?

あのレストラン
**ano resutoran**
(an-oh res-toh-run)

And how would you say "I ate sushi in that restaurant"?

あのレストランですしを食べました。
**Ano resutoran de sushi o tabemashita.**
(an-oh res-toh-run day sushi o ta-bay-mash-ta)

As I mentioned just a moment ago, "yesterday" in Japanese is:

昨日
**kinō**
(kee-noh)

So how would you say "Yesterday, I ate sushi in that restaurant"?

昨日、あのレストランですしを食べました。
**Kinō, ano resutoran de sushi o tabemashita.**
(kee-noh an-oh res-toh-run day sushi o ta-bay-mash-ta)

And how would you say "Yesterday, I ate katsu curry in that restaurant"?

昨日、あのレストランでカツカレーを食べました。
**Kinō, ano resutoran de katsu karē o tabemashita.**
(kee-noh an-oh res-toh-run day kats ka-ray o ta-bay-mash-ta)

By the way, it's a good idea in Japanese to put when you did something – in this case, *yesterday* – right at the front of the sentence. So, no matter what order you put the words in English – whether you're saying "*yesterday*, I ate katsu curry in that restaurant" or "I ate katsu curry in that restaurant *yesterday*" – in Japanese, simply put the "yesterday" right up at the front and that way your Japanese will always be correct.

So, with that in mind, how would you say "I ate katsu curry in that restaurant yesterday"?

昨日、あのレストランでカツカレーを食べました。
**Kinō, ano resutoran de katsu karē o tabemashita.**
(kee-noh an-oh res-toh-run day kats ka-ray o ta-bay-mash-ta)

With that, you've just constructed the sentence that we started the chapter with – and, as you will soon discover, this is only the very beginning of our journey into Japanese!

You just learnt how to say (amongst other things) "I ate katsu curry in that restaurant". Having done this, we are now going to move on to expand what you can say through the use of additional "building blocks".

The new building blocks you are going to learn will allow you to begin instantly expanding your range of expression in the Japanese language.

So far, some of the building blocks you have already learned include:

And you already know how to use these building blocks to construct a sentence. So, once again, how would you say "Yesterday, I ate in that restaurant"?

So, you already know how to build the four building blocks above into a sentence. Take a look now at six new building blocks below. Just have a glance over them and then I'll show you how we're going to add these into the mix of what we've learned so far.

食べました
tabemashita
(ta-bay-mash-ta)
she ate

うどん
udon
(oo-don)
udon

昨日の午後
Kinō no gogo[2]
(kee-noh noh goh-goh)
yesterday

食べました
tabemashita
(ta-bay-mash-ta)
he ate

天ぷら
tenpura
(ten-poo-ra)
tempura

昨日の晩
kinō no ban[3]
(kee-noh noh ban)
last night / yesterday evening

Okay, first things first: please don't try to memorise these words. No, no, no! Instead, I simply want you to play with your building blocks. After all, that's what building blocks are for, isn't it?

And the way you're going to play with them is like this: on the next page they have been put into five piles and all I want you to do is to make sentences with them. **You'll do this by each time using one building block from the first pile, one from the second, one from the third, one from the fourth and one from the fifth.**

You will find that you can say a lot of different things using them in this way and it's up to you what sentences you make. The only thing I want you to make sure you do is to use every building block at least once and, also, please don't bother writing down the sentences you make. Instead, say them out loud, or, if you're not in a place where you can do this, say them in your head. Now, off you go; make as many sentences as you can!

---

2   "Kinō no gogo" can be literally translated as "yesterday's afternoon". "Kinō" of course means "yesterday" in Japanese and "gogo" means "afternoon". The little word between "kinō" and "gogo" – "no" – more or less has the same meaning as an apostrophe followed by an "s" in English, the same meaning as: **'s**. So, for instance, if you wanted to say "Paul's sushi" in Japanese, you'd say "Paul **no** sushi". If you wanted to say "Susan**'s** restaurant" you'd say "Susan **no** restaurant". So "**no**" in Japanese = **'s**. And that's why "kinō **no** gogo" literally means "yesterday**'s** afternoon"!

3   "Kinō **no** ban" can be literally translated as "yesterday**'s** evening".

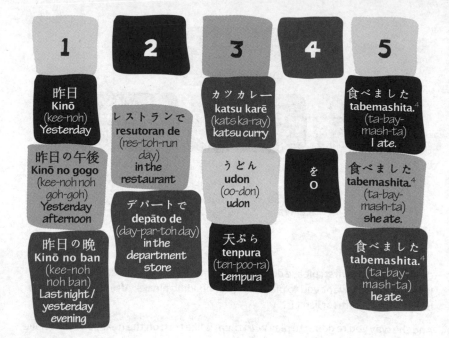

**1**

昨日
Kinō
(kee-noh)
Yesterday

昨日の午後
Kinō no gogo
(kee-noh noh goh-goh)
Yesterday afternoon

昨日の晩
Kinō no ban
(kee-noh noh ban)
Last night / yesterday evening

**2**

レストランで
resutoran de
(res-toh-run day)
in the restaurant

デパートで
depāto de
(day-par-toh day)
in the department store

**3**

カツカレー
katsu karē
(kats ka-ray)
katsu curry

うどん
udon
(oo-don)
udon

天ぷら
tenpura
(ten-poo-ra)
tempura

**4**

を
O

**5**

食べました
tabemashita.[4]
(ta-bay-mash-ta)
I ate.

食べました
tabemashita.[4]
(ta-bay-mash-ta)
she ate.

食べました
tabemashita.[4]
(ta-bay-mash-ta)
he ate.

## The Checklist

You have now reached the final part of Chapter One. Once you have finished this short section you will not only have completed your first chapter but you will also understand how this book works as the other chapters follow the same pattern, with your Japanese getting ever more sophisticated as you complete each chapter.

The section you are now on will be the final part of each chapter and is what I call "The Checklist". It involves nothing more than a read-through of a selection of some of the words or expressions you have so far encountered.

You will actually see the checklist twice. The first time you will see that the Japanese words are written in black (on the left-hand side) and that the English words are written in **red** (on the right-hand side) – and you know what red means! Cover up!

---

4    Yep, you read that correctly: "I ate", "she ate" and "he ate" are all said in the exact same way in Japanese. There's no difference between them. Japanese speakers know which one is being said simply through context. This is something you'll also get used to doing.

So, what I want you to do here is to cover up the English words (which are written in red on the right-hand side) while you read through the list of Japanese words on the left. Read through them all, from the top of the list to the bottom, and see if you can recall what they mean in English (uncover one red word at a time to check if you've remembered the meaning correctly). If you can go through the entire list, giving the correct English meaning for each of the Japanese words / expressions **without making more than 3 mistakes in total**, then you're done.

If not, then go through the list again. Keep doing this, either working from the top of the list to bottom or from the bottom to the top (it doesn't matter which) until you can do it **without making more than 3 mistakes**.

Got it? Then let's go!

| | |
|---|---|
| 東京<br>**Tōkyō**<br>(toh-kee-oh) | Tokyo |
| に<br>**ni**<br>(nee) | to |
| 東京に<br>**Tōkyō ni**<br>(toh-kee-oh nee) | to Tokyo |
| 行きました<br>**ikimashita**<br>(ik-ee-mash-ta) | I went |
| レストラン<br>resutoran<br>(res-toh-run) | restaurant / the restaurant / a restaurant |
| レストランに行きました。<br>**Resutoran ni ikimashita.**<br>(res-toh-run nee ik-ee-mash-ta) | I went to the restaurant. |
| と<br>**to**<br>(to) | with |
| Paulと<br>**Paul to**<br>(paul to) | with Paul |

|  |  |
|---|---|
| Paulとレストランに行きました。<br>**Paul to resutoran ni ikimashita.**<br>(paul to res-toh-run nee ik-ee-mash-ta) | I went to the restaurant with Paul. |
| Paulと東京に行きました。<br>**Paul to Tōkyō ni ikimashita.**<br>(paul to toh-kee-oh nee ik-ee-mash-ta) | I went to Tokyo with Paul. |
| デパート<br>**depāto**<br>(day-par-toh) | department store / the department store / a department store |
| さん<br>**san**<br>(sun) | Mr / Mrs / Ms |
| 鈴木さん<br>**Suzuki san**<br>(su-zoo-kee sun) | Mr Suzuki / Mrs Suzuki / Ms Suzuki |
| 鈴木さんとデパートに行きました。<br>**Suzuki san to depāto ni ikimashita.**<br>(su-zoo-kee sun to day-par-toh nee ik-ee-mash-ta) | I went to the department store with Ms Suzuki. |
| 食べました<br>**tabemashita**<br>(ta-bay-mash-ta) | I ate |
| Paulと食べました。<br>**Paul to tabemashita.**<br>(paul to ta-bay-mash-ta) | I ate with Paul. |
| すし<br>**sushi**<br>(sushi) | sushi |
| を<br>**o**<br>(o) | *The word that you put after the thing that's been eaten.* |
| すしを食べました。<br>**Sushi o tabemashita.**<br>(sushi o ta-bay-mash-ta) | I ate sushi. |

| 鈴木さんとすしを食べました。<br>**Suzuki san to sushi o tabemashita.**<br>(su-zoo-kee sun to sushi o ta-bay-mash-ta) | I ate sushi with Mr Suzuki. |
| ラーメン<br>**rāmen**<br>(ra-men) | ramen / noodle soup |
| 鈴木さんとラーメンを食べました。<br>**Suzuki san to rāmen o tabemashita.**<br>(su-zoo-kee sun to ra-men o ta-bay-mash-ta) | I ate ramen with Mrs Suzuki. |
| で<br>**de**<br>(day) | in |
| レストランで<br>**resutoran de**<br>(res-toh-run day) | in the restaurant |
| 鈴木さんとレストランでラーメンを食べました。<br>**Suzuki san to resutoran de rāmen o tabemashita.**<br>(su-zoo-kee sun to res-toh-run day ra-men o ta-bay-mash-ta) | I ate ramen with Mrs Suzuki in the restaurant. |
| カツカレー<br>**katsu karē**<br>(kats ka-ray) | katsu curry |
| 田中さん<br>**Tanaka san**<br>(ta-na-ka sun) | Mr Tanaka / Mrs Tanaka / Ms Tanaka |
| 田中さんとレストランでカツカレーを食べました。<br>**Tanaka san to resutoran de katsu karē o tabemashita.**<br>(ta-na-ka sun to res-toh-run day kats ka-ray o ta-bay-mash-ta) | I ate katsu curry in the restaurant with Mr Tanaka. |

| | |
|---|---|
| デパートで<br>**depāto de**<br>(day-par-toh day) | in the department store |
| 田中さんとデパートでカツカレーを食べました。<br>**Tanaka san to depāto de katsu karē o tabemashita.**<br>(ta-na-ka sun to day-par-toh day kats ka-ray o tab-ay-mash-ta) | I ate katsu curry in the department store with Ms Tanaka. |
| あのデパート<br>**ano depāto**<br>(an-oh day-par-toh) | that department store |
| あのデパートで<br>**ano depāto de**<br>(an-oh day-par-toh day) | in that department store |
| 田中さんとあのデパートでカツカレーを食べました。<br>**Tanaka san to ano depāto de katsu karē o tabemashita.**<br>(ta-na-ka sun to an-oh de-par-toh day kats ka-ray o tab-ay-mash-ta) | I ate katsu curry in that department store with Ms Tanaka. |
| あのレストラン<br>**ano resutoran**<br>(an-oh res-toh-run) | that restaurant |
| あのレストランで<br>**ano resutoran de**<br>(an-oh res-toh-run day) | in that restaurant |
| 昨日<br>**kinō**<br>(kee-noh) | yesterday |
| 昨日、食べました<br>**kinō, tabemashita**<br>(kee-noh ta-bay-mash-ta) | yesterday, I ate |

| | |
|---|---|
| 昨日、鈴木さんとあのレストランでラーメンを食べました。<br>**Kinō, Suzuki san to ano resutoran de rāmen o tabemashita.**<br>(kee-noh su-zoo-kee sun to an-oh res-toh-run day ra-men o ta-bay-mash-ta) | Yesterday, I ate ramen in that restaurant with Mrs Suzuki. |
| 昨日の午後<br>**kinō no gogo**<br>(kee-noh noh goh-goh) | yesterday afternoon (literally "yesterday's afternoon") |
| 昨日の午後、鈴木さんと東京に行きました。<br>**Kinō no gogo, Suzuki san to Tōkyō ni ikimashita.**<br>(kee-noh noh goh-goh su-zoo-kee sun to toh-kee-oh nee ik-ee-mash-ta) | Yesterday afternoon, I went to Tokyo with Mrs Suzuki. |
| あのレストランに<br>**ano resutoran ni**<br>(an-oh res-toh-run nee) | to that restaurant |
| 昨日の晩<br>**kinō no ban**<br>(kee-noh noh ban) | yesterday evening / last night (literally "yesterday's evening") |
| 昨日の晩、田中さんとあのレストランに行きました。<br>**Kinō no ban, Tanaka san to ano resutoran ni ikimashita.**<br>(kee-noh noh ban ta-na-ka sun to res-toh-run nee ik-ee-mash-ta) | Yesterday evening, I went to that restaurant with Ms Tanaka. |
| 天ぷら<br>**tenpura**<br>(ten-poo-ra) | tempura |
| 食べました<br>**tabemashita**<br>(ta-bay-mash-ta) | she ate |
| 天ぷらを食べました。<br>**Tenpura o tabemashita.**<br>(ten-poo-ra o ta-bay-mash-ta) | She ate tempura. |

|  |  |
|---|---|
| レストランで天ぷらを食べました。<br>**Resutoran de tenpura o tabemashita.**<br>(res-toh-run day ten-poo-ra o ta-bay-mash-ta) | She ate tempura in the restaurant. |
| あのレストランで天ぷらを食べました。<br>**Ano resutoran de tenpura o tabemashita.**<br>(an-oh res-toh-run day ten-poo-ra o ta-bay-mash-ta) | She ate tempura in that restaurant. |
| うどん<br>**udon**<br>(oo-don) | udon |
| 食べました<br>**tabemashita**<br>(ta-bay-mash-ta) | he ate |
| うどんを食べました。<br>**Udon o tabemashita.**<br>(oo-don o ta-bay-mash-ta) | He ate udon. |
| デパートでうどんを食べました。<br>**Depāto de udon o tabemashita.**<br>(day-par-toh day oo-don o ta-bay-mash-ta) | He ate udon in the department store. |
| あのデパートでうどんを食べました。<br>**Ano depāto de udon o tabemashita.**<br>(an-oh day-par-toh day oo-don o ta-bay-mash-ta) | He ate udon in that department store. |
| 昨日の午後、田中さんとあのデパートでうどんを食べました。<br>**Kinō no gogo, Tanaka san to ano depāto de udon o tabemashita.**<br>(kee-noh noh goh-goh ta-na-ka sun to an-oh day-par-toh day oo-don o ta-bay-mash-ta) | Yesterday afternoon, he ate udon in that department store with Mr Tanaka. |

Finished working through that checklist and made less than 3 mistakes?
Yes? Wonderful!

As that's the case, what I want you to do now is to repeat exactly the same process again below, except that this time you'll be reading through the *English* and trying to recall the Japanese. So, it will be the other way around. So, just relax and work your way up and down the list until you can give the correct Japanese translation for each of the English words / expressions again **without making more than 3 mistakes in total**. It's not a competition – and I'm not asking you to memorise them. No! Just look at the English words (on the left-hand side) while you cover up the red Japanese words on the right-hand side and see if you can remember how to say them in Japanese. You'll be surprised by how much you get right, even on the first try!

## Okay, off you go!

| | |
|---|---|
| Tokyo | 東京<br>**Tōkyō**<br>(toh-kee-oh) |
| to | に<br>**ni**<br>(nee) |
| to Tokyo | 東京に<br>**Tōkyō ni**<br>(toh-kee-oh nee) |
| I went | 行きました<br>**ikimashita**<br>(ik-ee-mash-ta) |
| restaurant / the restaurant / a restaurant | レストラン<br>**resutoran**<br>(res-toh-run) |
| I went to the restaurant. | レストランに行きました。<br>**Resutoran ni ikimashita.**<br>(res-toh-run nee ik-ee-mash-ta) |
| with | と<br>**to**<br>(to) |
| with Paul | Paulと<br>**Paul to**<br>(paul to) |

| | |
|---|---|
| I went to the restaurant with Paul. | Paulとレストランに行きました。<br>**Paul to resutoran ni ikimashita.**<br>(paul to res-toh-run nee ik-ee-mash-ta) |
| I went to Tokyo with Paul. | Paulと東京に行きました。<br>**Paul to Tōkyō ni ikimashita.**<br>(paul to toh-kee-oh nee ik-ee-mash-ta) |
| department store / the department store / a department store | デパート<br>**depāto**<br>(day-par-toh) |
| Mr / Mrs / Ms | さん<br>**san**<br>(sun) |
| Mr Suzuki / Mrs Suzuki / Ms Suzuki | 鈴木さん<br>**Suzuki san**<br>(su-zoo-kee sun) |
| I went to the department store with Ms Suzuki. | 鈴木さんとデパートに行きました。<br>**Suzuki san to depāto ni ikimashita.**<br>(su-zoo-kee sun to day-par-toh nee ik-ee-mash-ta) |
| I ate | 食べました<br>**tabemashita**<br>(ta-bay-mash-ta) |
| I ate with Paul. | Paulと食べました。<br>**Paul to tabemashita.**<br>(paul to ta-bay-mash-ta) |
| sushi | すし<br>**sushi**<br>(sushi) |
| *The word that you put after the thing that's been eaten.* | を<br>**o**<br>(o) |
| I ate sushi. | すしを食べました。<br>**Sushi o tabemashita.**<br>(sushi o ta-bay-mash-ta) |

| | |
|---|---|
| I ate sushi with Mr Suzuki. | 鈴木さんとすしを食べました。<br>**Suzuki san to sushi o tabemashita.**<br>(su-zoo-kee sun to sushi o ta-bay-mash-ta) |
| ramen / noodle soup | ラーメン<br>**rāmen**<br>(ra-men) |
| I ate ramen with Mrs Suzuki. | 鈴木さんとラーメンを食べました。<br>**Suzuki san to rāmen o tabemashita.**<br>(su-zoo-kee sun to ra-men o ta-bay-mash-ta) |
| in | で<br>**de**<br>(day) |
| in the restaurant | レストランで<br>**resutoran de**<br>(res-toh-run day) |
| I ate ramen with Mrs Suzuki in the restaurant. | 鈴木さんとデパートでラーメンを食べました。<br>**Suzuki san to resutoran de rāmen o tabemashita.**<br>(su-zoo-kee sun to res-toh-run day ra-men o ta-bay-mash-ta) |
| katsu curry | カツカレー<br>**katsu karē**<br>(kats ka-ray) |
| Mr Tanaka / Mrs Tanaka / Ms Tanaka | 田中さん<br>**Tanaka san**<br>(ta-na-ka sun) |
| I ate katsu curry in the restaurant with Mr Tanaka. | 田中さんとレストランでカツカレーを食べました。<br>**Tanaka san to resutoran de katsu karē o tabemashita.**<br>(ta-na-ka sun to res-toh-run day kats ka-ray o ta-bay-mash-ta) |

| | |
|---|---|
| in the department store | デパートで<br>**depāto de**<br>(day-par-toh day) |
| I ate katsu curry in the department store with Ms Tanaka. | 田中さんとデパートでカツカレーを食べました。<br>**Tanaka san to depāto de katsu karē o tabemashita.**<br>(ta-na-ka sun to day-par-toh day kats ka-ray o ta-bay-mash-ta) |
| that department store | あのデパート<br>**ano depāto**<br>(an-oh day-par-toh) |
| in that department store | あのデパートで<br>**ano depāto de**<br>(an-oh day-par-toh day) |
| I ate katsu curry in that department store with Ms Tanaka. | 田中さんとあのデパートでカツカレーを食べました。<br>**Tanaka san to ano depāto de katsu karē o tabemashita.**<br>(ta-na-ka sun to an-oh day-par-toh day kats ka-ray o ta-bay-mash-ta) |
| that restaurant | あのレストラン<br>**ano resutoran**<br>(an-oh res-toh-run) |
| in that restaurant | あのレストランで<br>**ano resutoran de**<br>(an-oh res-toh-run day) |
| yesterday | 昨日<br>**kinō**<br>(kee-noh) |
| yesterday, I ate | 昨日、食べました<br>**kinō, tabemashita**<br>(kee-noh ta-bay-mash-ta) |
| Yesterday, I ate ramen in that restaurant with Mrs Suzuki. | 昨日、鈴木さんとあのレストランでラーメンを食べました。<br>**Kinō, Suzuki san to ano resutoran de rāmen o tabemashita.**<br>(kee-noh su-zoo-kee sun to an-oh res-toh-run day ra-men o ta-bay-mash-ta) |

| | |
|---|---|
| yesterday afternoon (literally "yesterday's afternoon") | 昨日の午後<br>**kinō no gogo**<br>(kee-noh noh goh-goh) |
| Yesterday afternoon, I went to Tokyo with Mrs Suzuki. | 昨日の午後、鈴木さんと東京に行きました。<br>**Kinō no gogo, Suzuki san to Tōkyō ni ikimashita.**<br>(kee-noh noh goh-goh su-zoo-kee sun to toh-kee-oh nee ik-ee-mash-ta) |
| to that restaurant | あのレストランに<br>**ano resutoran ni**<br>(an-oh res-toh-run nee) |
| yesterday evening / last night (literally "yesterday's evening") | 昨日の晩<br>**kinō no ban**<br>(kee-noh noh ban) |
| Yesterday evening, I went to that restaurant with Ms Tanaka. | 昨日の晩、田中さんとあのレストランに行きました。<br>**Kinō no ban, Tanaka san to ano resutoran ni ikimashita.**<br>(kee-noh noh ban ta-na-ka sun to res-toh-run nee ik-ee-mash-ta) |
| tempura | 天ぷら<br>**tenpura**<br>(ten-poo-ra) |
| she ate | 食べました<br>**tabemashita**<br>(ta-bay-mash-ta) |
| She ate tempura. | 天ぷらを食べました。<br>**Tenpura o tabemashita.**<br>(ten-poo-ra o ta-bay-mash-ta) |
| She ate tempura in the restaurant. | レストランで天ぷらを食べました。<br>**Resutoran de tenpura o tabemashita.**<br>(res-toh-run day ten-poo-ra o ta-bay-mash-ta) |

| | |
|---|---|
| She ate tempura in that restaurant. | あのレストランで天ぷらを食べました。<br>**Ano resutóran de tenpura o tabemashita.**<br>(an-oh res-toh-run day ten-poo-ra o ta-bay-mash-ta) |
| udon | うどん<br>**udon**<br>(oo-don) |
| he ate | 食べました<br>**tabemashita.**<br>(ta-bay-mash-ta) |
| He ate udon. | うどんを食べました。<br>**Udon o tabemashita.**<br>(oo-don o ta-bay-mash-ta) |
| He ate udon in the department store. | デパートでうどんを食べました。<br>**Depāto de udon o tabemashita.**<br>(day-par-toh day oo-don o ta-bay-mash-ta) |
| He ate udon in that department store. | あのデパートでうどんを食べました。<br>**Ano depāto de udon o tabemashita.**<br>(an-oh day-par-toh day oo-don o ta-bay-mash-ta) |
| Yesterday afternoon, he ate udon in that department store with Mr Tanaka. | 昨日の午後、田中さんとあのデパートでうどんを食べました。<br>**Kinō no gogo, Tanaka san to ano depāto de udon o tabemashita.**<br>(kee-noh noh goh-goh ta-na-ka sun to an-oh day-par-toh day oo-don o ta-bay-mash-ta) |

Well, that's it, you're done with Chapter 1! Now, don't try to hold onto or remember anything you've learned here. Everything you learn in earlier chapters will be brought up again and reinforced in later chapters. You don't need to do anything extra or make any effort to memorise anything. The book has been organised so that it does that for you. Now, off you go now and have a rest. You've earned it!

Between chapters, I'm going to be giving you various tips on language learning. These will range from useful tips about the Japanese language itself to advice on how to fit learning a language in with your daily routine. Ready for the first one? Here it is!

## Tip Number One – Study (at least a little) every day!

Learning a language is like building a fire – if you don't tend to it, it will go out! So, once you have decided to learn a foreign language, you really should study it every day.

It doesn't have to be for a long time though. Just 5 or 10 minutes each day will be enough, so long as you keep it up. Doing these 5 or 10 minutes will stop you forgetting what you've already learned and, over time, will let you put more meat on the bones of what you're learning.

As for what counts towards those 5 or 10 minutes, well that's up to you. Whilst you're working with this book, I would recommend that your five or ten minutes should be spent here, learning with me. Once you're done here, however, your five or ten minutes could be spent using an audio course, watching a Japanese video online, chatting with a Japanese-speaking acquaintance or attending a class if you want to learn in a more formal setting. The important thing though is to make sure that you do a little every day!

# CHAPTER 2

We went to Hokkaido yesterday —
we ate miso ramen in Sapporo.
It was delicious!

The first chapter has shown you that you can learn how to build full and meaningful sentences in Japanese with relative ease. It also showed you how some Japanese words are already familiar to English speakers – and you'll meet more of these words here!

What was "I ate"?

食べました
**tabemashita**
(ta-bay-mash-ta)

And do you remember, from the building block section, what "tempura" is in Japanese?

天ぷら
**tenpura**
(ten-poo-ra)

And so how would you say "I ate tempura"?

てんぷらを食べました。
**Tenpura o tabemashita.**
(ten-poo-ra o ta-bay-mash-ta)

And do you remember, from the same building block section, how to say "she ate"?

食べました
**tabemashita**
(ta-bay-mash-ta)

And so how would you say "she ate tempura"?

天ぷらを食べました。
**Tenpura o tabemashita.**
(ten-poo-ra o ta-bay-mash-ta)

What is "yesterday afternoon"?

昨日の午後
**Kinō no gogo**
(kee-noh noh goh-goh[1])

So how would you say "she ate tempura yesterday afternoon"?

昨日の午後、天ぷらを食べました。
**Kinō no gogo, tenpura o tabemashita.**
(kee-noh noh goh-goh ten-poo-ra o ta-bay-mash-ta)

And how would you say "he ate udon yesterday afternoon"?

昨日の午後、うどんを食べました。
**Kinō no gogo, udon o tabemashita.**
(kee-noh noh goh-goh oo-don o ta-bay-mash-ta)

You've already learned that "I ate", "he ate" and "she ate" are no different from one another in Japanese. Well, guess what: "we ate" is also the same! It is no different from "I ate", "he ate" or "she ate".

Now that may of course lead you to wonder: how on earth do the Japanese know whether someone means "I ate" or "he ate" or "she ate" or "we ate" when they say "tabemashita"? Well, the answer is that they know simply through context. If you're talking about your mother and then say "tabemashita" the person you're speaking to will know that you mean "she ate." If you're talking about your brother and say "tabemashita" then the person you're speaking to will know you mean "he ate." So, for a Japanese person, it's not confusing at all. Anyway, don't spend too much time worrying or thinking about any of this, just be aware that "I ate", "he ate", "she ate", and "we ate" are all "tabemashita".

So, to ask a very obvious question, what is "we ate"?

食べました
**tabemashita**
(ta-bay-mash-ta)

And what is "yesterday evening" or "last night"?

昨日の晩
**kinō no ban**
(kee-noh noh ban)

---

1   By the way, just in case you weren't absolutely sure, when something is spelled with an "oh" in the pronunciation guidance, you should pronounce it just like the "oh" in "Oh dear!"

And so how would you say "Last night we ate udon"?

昨日の晩、うどんを食べました。
**Kinō no ban, udon o tabemashita.**
(kee-noh noh ban oo-don o ta-bay-mash-ta)

What is "I went"?

行きました
**ikimashita**
(ik-ee-mash-ta)

Do you think you can guess how you'd say "*she* went"?

行きました
**ikimashita**
(ik-ee-mash-ta)

Yes, correct! Just as "I ate", "he ate" and "she ate" are the same as one another, so "I went" and "she went" are also the same. And, actually, can you guess how you'd say "he went"?

行きました
**ikimashita**
(ik-ee-mash-ta)

Yes, again, it's the same! In which case, why not make a lucky guess about how to say "we went". What do you think it will be?

行きました
**ikimashita**
(ik-ee-mash-ta)

Outstanding! You must be either a genius or clairvoyant to have worked that out! Or perhaps not...

Anyway, now that you know how to say "we went", how would you say "we went to Tokyo"?

東京に行きました。
**Tōkyō ni ikimashita.**
(toh-kee-oh nee ik-ee-mash-ta)

How about "we went to the restaurant"?

レストランに行きました。
**Resutoran ni ikimashita.**
(res-toh-run nee ik-ee-mash-ta)

How would you say "*that* restaurant"?

あのレストラン
**ano resutoran**
(an-oh res-toh-run)

And so how would you say "we went to that restaurant"?

あのレストランに行きました。
**Ano resutoran ni ikimashita.**
(an-oh res-toh-run nee ik-ee-mash-ta)

How about "we went to that restaurant yesterday afternoon"?

昨日の午後、あのレストランに行きました。
**Kinō no gogo, ano resutoran ni ikimashita.**
(kee-noh noh goh-goh an-oh res-toh-run nee ik-ee-mash-ta)

## The many islands of Japan...

Did you know that Japan is made up of almost seven thousand islands, some tiny and some very large? The largest islands are **Honshu** in the centre, **Kysuhu** and **Shikoku** in the south and **Hokkaido** in the north. There's also the important, sub tropical island of **Okinawa**, in the *very* far south. As it is sub-tropical, Okinawa is somewhere that you may want to go if you fancy a day at the beach during your visit to Japan...

So how would you say "I went to Okinawa"?

沖縄に行きました。
**Okinawa ni ikimashita.**
(ok-ee-now-a nee ik-ee-mash-ta)

And how about "we went to Okinawa"?

沖縄に行きました。
**Okinawa ni ikimashita.**
(ok-ee-now-a *nee* ik-ee-mash-ta)

What about "we went to Hokkaido"?

北海道に行きました。
**Hokkaidō ni ikimashita.**[2]
(ho-kai-doh *nee* ik-ee-mash-ta)

Now again, what is "the restaurant"?

レストラン
**resutoran**
(res-toh-run)

And do you remember how to say "in the restaurant"?

レストランで
**resutoran de**
(res-toh-run *day*)

How about "in the department store"?

デパートで
**depāto de**
(day-par-toh *day*)

So how do you think you'd say "in Tokyo"?

東京で
**Tōkyō de**
(toh-kee-oh *day*)

---

2　In Japanese "Hokkaido" is pronounced in a very similar way to how it is in English. The main difference is that the "do" at the end is pronounced for longer in Japanese than it is in English. So, when you say it, let that "doh" sound at the end linger on your tongue just a touch longer than you would in English.

And so how would you say "I ate katsu curry in Tokyo"?

東京でカツカレーを食べました。
**Tōkyō de katsu karē o tabemashita.**
(toh-kee-oh day kats ka-ray o ta-bay-mash-ta)

What about "I ate sushi in Okinawa"?

沖縄ですしを食べました。
**Okinawa de sushi o tabemashita.**
(ok-ee-now-a day sushi o ta-bay-mash-ta)

And "I ate ramen in Hokkaido"?

北海道でラーメンを食べました。
**Hokkaidō de rāmen o tabemashita.**
(ho-kai-doh day ra-men o ta-bay-mash-ta)

## On the subject of ramen...

Actually, as we're on the subject of ramen, it's worth mentioning that you will come across many different types of ramen if you visit Japan. And the various types of ramen are actually categorised by the type of broth that is used to make the soup. The types of broth include those made from pork stock, salt and water, soya sauce and, one of the most popular, miso, which is made from fermented soya beans.

So how do you think you would you say, "I ate miso ramen"?

みそラーメンを食べました。
**Miso rāmen o tabemashita.**
(mee-soh ra-men o ta-bay-mash-ta)

How about "I ate miso ramen in Hokkaido yesterday"?

昨日、北海道でみそラーメンを食べました。
**Kinō, Hokkaidō de miso rāmen o tabemashita.**
(kee-noh ho-kai-doh day mee-soh ra-men o ta-bay-mash-ta)

The regional capital of Hokkaido is Sapporo and, actually, Sapporo is famous for having the best miso ramen in Japan.

So how would you say "in Saporro"?

札幌で
**Sapporo de**
(sa-po-roh day)

And how would you say "I ate miso ramen in Sapporo"?

札幌でみそラーメンを食べました。
**Sapporo de miso rāmen o tabemashita.**
(sa-po-roh day mee-soh ra-men o ta-bay-mash-ta)

What about, "we ate miso ramen in Sapporo yesterday"?

昨日、札幌でみそラーメンを食べました。
**Kinō, Sapporo de miso rāmen o tabemashita.**
(kee-noh sa-po-roh day mee-soh ra-men o ta-bay-mash-ta)

Now again, what is "we went"?

行きました
**ikimashita**
(ik-ee-mash-ta)

And so how would you say "Yesterday, we went to Hokkaido"?

昨日、北海道に行きました。
**Kinō, Hokkaidō ni ikimashita.**
(kee-noh ho-kai-doh nee ik-ee-mash-ta)

And how would you say "Yesterday, we went to Hokkaido. We ate miso ramen in Sapporo."?

昨日、北海道に行きました。札幌でラーメンを食べました。
**Kinō, Hokkaidō ni ikimashita. Sapporo de miso rāmen o tabemashita.**
(kee-noh ho-kai-doh nee ik-ee-mash-ta. sa-po-roh day mee-soh ra-men o ta-bay-mash-ta)

"It is" in Japanese is:

です
**desu**
(dess)

Now remind me, what is "restaurant" or "the restaurant"?

レストラン
**resutoran**
(res-toh-run)

"A restaurant" in Japanese is also:

レストラン
**resutoran**
(res-toh-run)

And, as I told you just a moment ago, "it is" in Japanese is:

です
**desu**
(dess)

So how would you say "it is a restaurant" (you'll literally say "a restaurant it is")?

レストランです。
**Resutoran desu.**
(res-toh-run dess)

What is "department store", "the department store" (and also "a department store")?

デパート
**depāto**
(day-par-toh)

And so how would you say "It's a department store"?

デパートです。
**Depāto desu.**
(day-par-toh dess)

And how would you say "it's sushi"?

すしです。
**Sushi desu.**
(sushi dess)

How about "it's miso ramen"?

みそラーメンです。
**Miso rāmen desu.**
(mee-soh ra-men dess)

If you want to say something like "it was delicious" in Japanese, you will actually literally say "was delicious it is". Yes, you will indeed sound like you're channeling Yoda.

Anyway, remind me, what is "it is"?

です
**desu**
(dess)

"Was delicious" in Japanese is:

おいしかった
**Oishikatta**
(oy-sh-ka-ta)

So how would you say "It was delicious" literally "was delicious it is"?

おいしかったです！
**Oishikatta desu!**
(oy-sh-ka-ta dess)

And how would you say "Last night, I ate sushi. It was delicious!"?

昨日の晩、すしを食べました。おいしかったです。
**Kinō no ban, sushi o tabemashita. Oishikatta desu!**
(kee-noh noh ban, sushi o ta-bay-mash-ta. oy-sh-ka-ta dess)

How about "yesterday afternoon, I ate katsu curry. It was delicious!"?

昨日の午後、カツカレーを食べました。おいしかったです。
**Kinō no gogo, katsu karē o tabemashita. Oishikatta desu!**
(kee-noh noh goh-goh, kats ka-ray o ta-bay-mash-ta. oy-sh-ka-ta dess)

How would you say "that restaurant"?

あのレストラン
**ano resutoran**
(an-oh res-toh-run)

And so how would you say "yesterday afternoon, I ate katsu curry in that restaurant"?

昨日の午後、あのレストランでカツカレーを食べました。
**Kinō no gogo, ano resutoran de katsu karē o tabemashita.**
(kee-noh noh goh-goh, an-on res-toh-run day kats ka-ray o ta-bay-mash-ta)

Again, what is "it is"?

です
**desu**
(dess)

And what is "was delicious"?

おいしかった
**Oishikatta**
(oy-sh-ka-ta)

And again how would you say "it was delicious"?

おいしかったです
**Oishikatta desu!**
(oy-sh-ka-ta dess)

And how would you say "yesterday afternoon, I ate katsu curry in that restaurant. It was delicious!"

昨日の午後、あのレストランでカツカレーを食べました。おいしかったです！
**Kinō no gogo, ano resutoran de katsu karē o tabemashita. Oishikatta desu!**
(kee-noh noh goh-goh, an-on res-toh-run day kats ka-ray o ta-bay-mash-ta. oy-sh-ka-ta dess)

And how would you say "yesterday afternoon, I ate katsu curry in Sapporo. It was delicious!"

昨日の午後、札幌でカツカレーを食べました。おいしかったです！
**Kinō no gogo, Sapporo de katsu karē o tabemashita. Oishikatta desu!**
(*kee-noh noh goh-goh, sa-po-roh day kats ka-ray o ta-bay-mash-ta. oy-sh-ka-ta dess*)

**Again, what is "I went"?**

行きました
**ikimashita**
(*ik-ee-mash-ta*)

**And what is "we went"?**

行きました
**ikimashita**
(*ik-ee-mash-ta*)

**And so how would you say "we went to Sapporo"?**

札幌に行きました。
**Sapporo ni ikimashita.**
(*sa-po-roh nee ik-ee-mash-ta*)

**How about "we went to Hokkaido"?**

北海道に行きました。
**Hokkaidō ni ikimashita.**
(*ho-kai-doh nee ik-ee-mash-ta*)

**And so how would you say "yesterday, we went to Hokkaido. We ate miso ramen in Sapporo."?**

昨日、北海道に行きました。札幌でみそラーメンを食べました。
**Kinō, Hokkaidō ni ikimashita. Sapporo de miso rāmen o tabemashita.**
(*kee-noh, ho-kai-doh nee ik-ee-mash-ta. sa-po-roh day mee-soh ra-men o ta-bay-mash-ta.*)

And, finally, how would you say "Yesterday, we went to Hokkaido. We ate miso ramen in Sapporo. It was delicious."

昨日、北海道に行きました。札幌でみそラーメンを食べました。おいしかったです！

**Kinō, Hokkaidō ni ikimashita. Sapporo de miso rāmen o tabemashita. Oishikatta desu!**

(kee-noh, ho-kai-doh nee ik-ee-mash-ta. sa-po-roh day mee-soh ra-men o ta-bay-mash-ta. oy-sh-ka-ta dess)

Well, you've now worked your way back to the sentence we started with and, although we are only at the end of the second chapter, you are already building long, complex sentences in Japanese and beginning to gain an insight into how this fascinating language works!

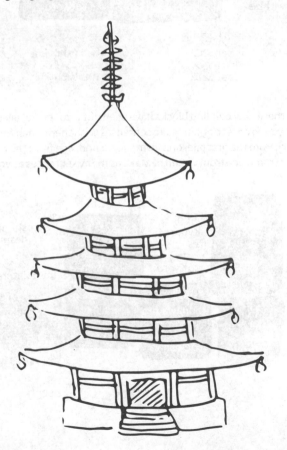

As before, it's time to add some new building blocks to the mix. Again, it will be just six new ones. Here they are:

Once more, these new building blocks have been put into several piles below and what I want you to do is to again make sentences with them, each time using one building block from the first pile, one from the second, one from the third, one from the fourth and one from the fifth. Make as many sentences as you can!

You have now reached your second checklist. Remember, don't skip anything! The checklists are essential if you want what you've learned to remain in your memory for the long term.

So again, cover up the English words on the right-hand side while you read through the list of Japanese words on the left, trying to recall what they mean in English. If you can go through the entire list, giving the correct English meaning for each of the Japanese words / expressions **without making more than 3 mistakes in total**, then you're done. If not, then go through the list again. Keep doing this, either working from the top of the list to the bottom or from the bottom to the top (it doesn't matter which) until you can do it **without making more than 3 mistakes**.

*Okay. Ready, set, go!*

| | |
|---|---|
| 東京<br>**Tōkyō**<br>(toh-kee-oh) | Tokyo |
| に<br>**ni**<br>(nee) | to |
| 東京に<br>**Tōkyō ni**<br>(toh-kee-oh nee) | to Tokyo |
| 行きました<br>**ikimashita**<br>(ik-ee-mash-ta) | I went |
| レストラン<br>**resutoran**<br>(res-toh-run) | restaurant / the restaurant /<br>a restaurant |
| レストランに行きました。<br>**Resutoran ni ikimashita.**<br>(res-toh-run nee ik-ee-mash-ta) | I went to the restaurant. |
| と<br>**to**<br>(to) | with |

|  |  |
|---|---|
| Paulと<br>**Paul to**<br>(paul to) | with Paul |
| Paulとレストランに行きました。<br>**Paul to resutoran ni ikimashita.**<br>(paul to res-toh-run nee ik-ee-<br>mash-ta) | I went to the restaurant with Paul. |
| Paulと東京に行きました。<br>**Paul to Tōkyō ni ikimashita.**<br>(paul to toh-kee-oh nee ik-ee-<br>mash-ta) | I went to Tokyo with Paul. |
| デパート<br>**depāto**<br>(day-par-toh) | department store /<br>the department store /<br>a department store |
| さん<br>**san**<br>(sun) | Mr / Mrs / Ms |
| 鈴木さん<br>**Suzuki san**<br>(su-zoo-kee sun) | Mr Suzuki / Mrs Suzuki / Ms Suzuki |
| 鈴木さんとデパートに行きました。<br>**Suzuki san to depāto ni ikimashita.**<br>(su-zoo-kee sun to day-par-toh nee<br>ik-ee-mash-ta) | I went to the department store<br>with Ms Suzuki. |
| 食べました<br>**tabemashita**<br>(ta-bay-mash-ta) | I ate |
| Paulと食べました。<br>**Paul to tabemashita.**<br>(paul to ta-bay-mash-ta) | I ate with Paul. |
| すし<br>**sushi**<br>(sushi) | sushi |
| を<br>**o**<br>(o) | *The word that you put after the thing<br>that's been eaten.* |

| | |
|---|---|
| すしを食べました。<br>**Sushi o tabemashita.**<br>(sushi o ta-bay-mash-ta) | I ate sushi. |
| 鈴木さんとすしを食べました。<br>**Suzuki san to sushi o tabemashita.**<br>(su-zoo-kee sun to sushi o ta-bay-mash-ta) | I ate sushi with Mr Suzuki. |
| ラーメン<br>**rāmen**<br>(ra-men) | ramen / noodle soup |
| 鈴木さんとラーメンを食べました。<br>**Suzuki san to rāmen o tabemashita.**<br>(su-zoo-kee sun to ra-men o ta-bay-mash-ta) | I ate ramen with Mrs Suzuki. |
| で<br>**de**<br>(day) | in |
| レストランで<br>**resutoran de**<br>(res-toh-run day) | in the restaurant |
| 鈴木さんとレストランでラーメンを食べました。<br>**Suzuki san to resutoran de rāmen o tabemashita.**<br>(su-zoo-kee sun to res-toh-run day ra-men o ta-bay-mash-ta) | I ate ramen with Mrs Suzuki in the restaurant. |
| カツカレー<br>**katsu karē**<br>(kats ka-ray) | katsu curry |
| 田中さん<br>**Tanaka san**<br>(ta-na-ka sun) | Mr Tanaka / Mrs Tanaka / Ms Tanaka |
| 田中さんとレストランでカツカレーを食べました。<br>**Tanaka san to resutoran de katsu karē o tabemashita.**<br>(ta-na-ka sun to res-toh-run day kats ka-ray o ta-bay-mash-ta) | I ate katsu curry in the restaurant with Mr Tanaka. |

| | |
|---|---|
| デパートで<br>**depāto de**<br>(day-par-toh day) | in the department store |
| 田中さんとデパートでカツカレ<br>ーを食べました。<br>**Tanaka san to depāto de katsu<br>karē o tabemashita.**<br>(ta-na-ka sun to day-par-toh day<br>kats ka-ray o ta-bay-mash-ta) | I ate katsu curry in the department<br>store with Ms Tanaka. |
| あのデパート<br>**ano depāto**<br>(an-oh day-par-toh) | that department store |
| あのデパートで<br>**ano depāto de**<br>(an-oh day-par-toh day) | in that department store |
| 田中さんとあのデパートでカツ<br>カレーを食べました。<br>**Tanaka san to ano depāto de katsu<br>karē o tabemashita.**<br>(ta-na-ka sun to an-oh de-par-<br>toh day kats ka-ray o tab-ay-<br>mash-ta) | I ate katsu curry in that<br>department store with Ms Tanaka. |
| あのレストラン<br>**ano resutoran**<br>(an-oh res-toh-run) | that restaurant |
| あのレストランで<br>**ano resutoran de**<br>(an-oh res-toh-run day) | in that restaurant |
| 昨日<br>**kinō**<br>(kee-noh) | yesterday |
| 昨日、食べました<br>**kinō, tabemashita**<br>(kee-noh ta-bay-mash-ta) | yesterday, I ate |

| | |
|---|---|
| 昨日、鈴木さんとあのデパートでラーメンを食べました。<br>**Kinō, Suzuki san to ano resutoran de rāmen o tabemashita.**<br>(kee-noh su-zoo-kee sun to an-oh res-toh-run day ra-men o ta-bay-mash-ta) | Yesterday, I ate ramen in that restaurant with Mrs Suzuki. |
| 昨日の午後<br>**kinō no gogo**<br>(kee-noh noh goh-goh) | yesterday afternoon (literally "yesterday's afternoon") |
| 昨日の午後、鈴木さんと東京に行きました。<br>**Kinō no gogo, Suzuki san to Tōkyō ni ikimashita.**<br>(kee-noh noh goh-goh su-zoo-kee sun to toh-kee-oh nee ik-ee-mash-ta) | Yesterday afternoon, I went to Tokyo with Mrs Suzuki. |
| あのレストランに<br>**ano resutoran ni**<br>(an-oh res-toh-run nee) | to that restaurant |
| 昨日の晩<br>**kinō no ban**<br>(kee-noh noh ban) | yesterday evening / last night (literally "yesterday's evening") |
| 昨日の晩、田中さんとあのレストランに行きました。<br>**Kinō no ban, Tanaka san to ano resutoran ni ikimashita.**<br>(kee-noh noh ban ta-na-ka sun to res-toh-run nee ik-ee-mash-ta) | Yesterday evening, I went to that restaurant with Ms Tanaka. |
| 天ぷら<br>**tenpura**<br>(ten-poo-ra) | tempura |
| 食べました<br>**tabemashita**<br>(ta-bay-mash-ta) | she ate |
| 天ぷらを食べました。<br>**Tenpura o tabemashita.**<br>(ten-poo-ra o ta-bay-mash-ta) | She ate tempura. |

| | |
|---|---|
| レストランで天ぷらを食べました。<br>**Resutoran de tenpura o tabemashita.**<br>(res-toh-run day ten-poo-ra o ta-bay-mash-ta) | She ate tempura in the restaurant. |
| あのレストランで天ぷらを食べました。<br>**Ano resutoran de tenpura o tabemashita.**<br>(an-oh res-toh-run day ten-poo-ra o ta-bay-mash-ta) | She ate tempura in that restaurant. |
| うどん<br>**udon**<br>(oo-don) | udon |
| 食べました<br>**tabemashita**<br>(ta-bay-mash-ta) | he ate |
| うどんを食べました。<br>**Udon o tabemashita.**<br>(oo-don o ta-bay-mash-ta) | He ate udon. |
| デパートでうどんを食べました。<br>**Depāto de udon o tabemashita.**<br>(day-par-toh day oo-don o ta-bay-mash-ta) | He ate udon in the department store. |
| あのデパートでうどんを食べました。<br>**Ano depāto de udon o tabemashita.**<br>(an-oh day-par-toh day oo-don o ta-bay-mash-ta) | He ate udon in that department store. |
| 昨日の午後、田中さんとあのデパートでうどんを食べました。<br>**Kinō no gogo, Tanaka san to ano depāto de udon o tabemashita.**<br>(kee-noh noh goh-goh ta-na-ka sun to an-oh day-par-toh day oo-don o ta-bay-mash-ta) | Yesterday afternoon, he ate udon in that department store with Mr Tanaka. |

| | |
|---|---|
| 食べました<br>**tabemashita**<br>(ta-bay-mash-ta) | we ate |
| うどんを食べました。<br>**Udon o tabemashita.**<br>(oo-don o ta-bay-mash-ta) | We ate udon. |
| 昨日の晩、うどんを食べました。<br>**Kinō no ban, udon o tabemashita.**<br>(kee-noh noh ban oo-don o ta-bay-mash-ta) | We ate udon last night. |
| 沖縄<br>**Okinawa**<br>(ok-ee-now-a) | Okinawa |
| 昨日の晩、沖縄でうどんを食べました。<br>**Kinō no ban, Okinawa de udon o tabemashita.**<br>(kee-noh noh ban ok-ee-now-a day oo-don o ta-bay-mash-ta) | We ate udon in Okinawa last night. |
| 行きました<br>**ikimashita**<br>(ik-ee-mash-ta) | she went |
| 行きました<br>**ikimashita.**<br>(ik-ee-mash-ta) | he went |
| 行きました<br>**ikimashita**<br>(ik-ee-mash-ta) | we went |
| 昨日の午後、あのレストランに行きました。<br>**Kinō no gogo, ano resutoran ni ikimashita.**<br>(kee-noh noh goh-goh an-oh res-toh-run nee ik-ee-mash-ta) | We went to that restaurant yesterday afternoon. |
| 北海道<br>**Hokkaidō**<br>(ho-kai-doh) | Hokkaido |

|  |  |
|---|---|
| 昨日、北海道に行きました。<br>**Kinō, Hokkaidō ni ikimashita.**<br>(kee-noh ho-kai-doh nee ik-ee-mash-ta.) | We went to Hokkaido yesterday. |
| 札幌<br>**Sapporo**<br>(sa-po-roh) | Sapporo |
| 札幌で食べました。<br>**Sapporo de tabemashita.**<br>(sa-po-roh day ta-bay-mash-ta) | We ate in Sapporo. |
| みそラーメン<br>**miso rāmen**<br>(mee-soh ra-men) | miso ramen |
| 札幌でみそラーメンを食べました。<br>**Sapporo de miso rāmen o tabemashita.**<br>(sa-po-roh day mee-soh ra-men o ta-bay-mash-ta) | We ate miso ramen in Sapporo. |
| 昨日、北海道に行きました。札幌でみそラーメンを食べました。<br>**Kinō, Hokkaidō ni ikimashita. Sapporo de miso rāmen o tabemashita.**<br>(kee-noh ho-kai-doh nee ik-ee-mash-ta. sa-po-roh day mee-soh ra-men o ta-bay-mash-ta) | We went to Hokkaido yesterday. We ate miso ramen in Sapporo. |
| です<br>**desu**<br>(dess) | it is |
| みそラーメンです。<br>**Miso rāmen desu.**<br>(mee-soh ra-men dess) | It's miso ramen. |
| デパートです。<br>**Depāto desu.**<br>(day-par-toh dess) | It's a department store. |

| | |
|---|---|
| おいしかった<br>**Oishikatta**<br>(oy-sh-ka-ta) | was delicious |
| おいしかったです！<br>**Oishikatta desu!**<br>(oy-sh-ka-ta dess) | It was delicious! |
| 昨日の午後、札幌でみそラーメンを食べました。おいしかったです！<br>**Kinō no gogo, Sapporo de miso rāmen o tabemashita. Oishikatta desu!**<br>(kee-noh noh goh-goh, sa-po-roh day mee-soh ra-men o ta-bay-mash-ta. oy-sh-ka-ta dess) | Yesterday afternoon, I ate miso ramen in Sapporo. It was delicious! |
| 昨日、北海道に行きました。札幌でみそラーメンを食べました。おいしかったです！<br>**Kinō, Hokkaidō ni ikimashita. Sapporo de miso rāmen o tabemashita. Oishikatta desu!**<br>(kee-noh, ho-kai-doh nee ik-ee-mash-ta. sa-po-roh day mee-soh ra-men o ta-bay-mash-ta. oy-sh-ka-ta dess) | Yesterday, we went to Hokkaido. We ate miso ramen in Sapporo. It was delicious. |
| 行きました<br>**ikimashita**<br>(ik-ee-mash-ta) | they went |
| 京都に<br>**Kyōto ni**<br>(kee-oh-toh nee) | to Kyoto |
| 京都に行きました。<br>**Kyōto ni ikimashita.**<br>(kee-oh-toh nee ik-ee-mash-ta) | They went to Kyoto. |
| 私と<br>**watashi to**<br>(wa-ta-sh to) | with me |

| | |
|---|---|
| 私と京都に行きました。<br>**Watashi to Kyōto ni ikimashita.**<br>(wa-ta-sh to kee-oh-toh nee ik-ee-<br>mash-ta) | They went to Kyoto with me. |
| 先週<br>**sen shū**<br>(sen shoo) | last week |
| 先週、私と京都に行きました。<br>**Sen shū, watashi to Kyōto ni<br>ikimashita.**<br>(sen shoo, wa-ta-sh to kee-oh-toh<br>nee ik-ee-mash-ta) | Last week, they went to Kyoto<br>with me. |
| 面白かった<br>**omoshirokatta**<br>(om-osh-ee-ro-ka-ta) | was interesting |
| 面白かったです！<br>**Omoshirokatta desu!**<br>(om-osh-ee-ro-ka-ta dess) | It was interesting! |
| 先週、田中さんと京都に行きま<br>した。面白かったです。<br>**Sen shū, Tanaka san to Kyōto ni<br>ikimashita. Omoshirokatta desu.**<br>(sen shoo, ta-na-ka sun to kee-oh-<br>toh nee ik-ee-mash-ta. om-osh-ee-<br>ro-ka-ta dess) | Last week, we went to Kyoto with<br>Mrs Tanaka. It was interesting. |
| 美しかった<br>**utsukushikatta**<br>(oo-tsoo-koo-shee-ka-ta) | was beautiful |
| 美しかったです！<br>**Utsukushikatta desu!**<br>(oo-tsoo-koo-shee-ka-ta dess) | It was beautiful! |
| 先週、田中さんと沖縄に行きま<br>した。美しかったです。<br>**Sen shū, Tanaka san to Okinawa ni<br>ikimashita. Utsukushikatta desu!**<br>(sen shoo, ta-na-ka sun to ok-ee-<br>now-a nee ik-ee-mash-ta. oo-tsoo-<br>koo-shee-ka-ta dess) | Last week, we went to Okinawa with<br>Mrs Tanaka. It was beautiful. |

Now, once more, do the same thing again below, except that this time you'll be reading through the list of English words and trying to recall the Japanese. All you need to do is to be able to do one full read-through of them without making more than 3 mistakes in total and you're done!

| | |
|---|---|
| Tokyo | 東京<br>**Tōkyō**<br>(toh-kee-oh) |
| to | に<br>**ni**<br>(nee) |
| to Tokyo | 東京に<br>**Tōkyō ni**<br>(toh-kee-oh nee) |
| I went | 行きました<br>**ikimashita**<br>(ik-ee-mash-ta) |
| restaurant / the restaurant /<br>a restaurant | レストラン<br>**resutoran**<br>(res-toh-run) |
| I went to the restaurant. | レストランに行きました。<br>**Resutoran ni ikimashita.**<br>(res-toh-run nee ik-ee-mash-ta) |
| with | と<br>**to**<br>(to) |
| with Paul | Paulと<br>**Paul to**<br>(paul to) |
| I went to the restaurant with Paul. | Paulとレストランに行きました。<br>**Paul to resutoran ni ikimashita.**<br>(paul to res-toh-run nee<br>ik-ee-mash-ta) |
| I went to Tokyo with Paul. | Paulと東京に行きました。<br>**Paul to Tōkyō ni ikimashita.**<br>(paul to toh-kee-oh nee<br>ik-ee-mash-ta) |

| | |
|---|---|
| department store / the department store / a department store | デパート<br>**depāto**<br>(day-par-toh) |
| Mr / Mrs / Ms | さん<br>**san**<br>(sun) |
| Mr Suzuki / Mrs Suzuki / Ms Suzuki | 鈴木さん<br>**Suzuki san**<br>(su-zoo-kee sun) |
| I went to the department store with Ms Suzuki. | 鈴木さんとデパートに行きました。<br>**Suzuki san to depāto ni ikimashita.**<br>(su-zoo-kee sun to day-par-toh nee ik-ee-mash-ta) |
| I ate | 食べました<br>**tabemashita**<br>(ta-bay-mash-ta) |
| I ate with Paul. | Paulと食べました。<br>**Paul to tabemashita.**<br>(paul to ta-bay-mash-ta) |
| sushi | すし<br>**sushi**<br>(sushi) |
| *The word that you put after the thing that's been eaten.* | を<br>**o**<br>(o) |
| I ate sushi. | すしを食べました。<br>**Sushi o tabemashita.**<br>(sushi o ta-bay-mash-ta) |
| I ate sushi with Mr Suzuki. | 鈴木さんとすしを食べました。<br>**Suzuki san to sushi o tabemashita.**<br>(su-zoo-kee sun to sushi o ta-bay-mash-ta) |
| ramen / noodle soup | ラーメン<br>**rāmen**<br>(ra-men) |

| | |
|---|---|
| I ate ramen with Mrs Suzuki. | 鈴木さんとラーメンを食べました。<br>**Suzuki san to rāmen o tabemashita.**<br>(su-zoo-kee sun to ra-men o ta-bay-mash-ta) |
| in | で<br>**de**<br>(day) |
| in the restaurant | レストランで<br>**resutoran de**<br>(res-toh-run day) |
| I ate ramen with Mrs Suzuki in the restaurant. | 鈴木さんとレストランでラーメンを食べました。<br>**Suzuki san to resutoran de rāmen o tabemashita.**<br>(su-zoo-kee sun to res-toh-run day ra-men o ta-bay-mash-ta) |
| katsu curry | カツカレー<br>**katsu karē**<br>(kats ka-ray) |
| Mr Tanaka / Mrs Tanaka / Ms Tanaka | 田中さん<br>**Tanaka san**<br>(ta-na-ka sun) |
| I ate katsu curry in the restaurant with Mr Tanaka. | 田中さんとレストランでカツカレーを食べました。<br>**Tanaka san to resutoran de katsu karē o tabemashita.**<br>(ta-na-ka sun to res-toh-run day kats ka-ray o ta-bay-mash-ta) |
| in the department store | デパートで<br>**depāto de**<br>(day-par-toh day) |
| I ate katsu curry in the department store with Ms Tanaka. | 田中さんとデパートでカツカレーを食べました。<br>**Tanaka san to depāto de katsu karē o tabemashita.**<br>(ta-na-ka sun to day-par-toh day kats ka-ray o ta-bay-mash-ta) |

| | |
|---|---|
| that department store | あのデパート<br>**ano depāto**<br>*(an-oh day-par-toh)* |
| in that department store | あのデパートで<br>**ano depāto de**<br>*(an-oh day-par-toh day)* |
| I ate katsu curry in that department store with Ms Tanaka. | 田中さんとあのデパートでカツカレーを食べました。<br>**Tanaka san to ano depāto de katsu karē o tabemashita.**<br>*(ta-na-ka sun to an-oh day-par-toh day kats ka-ray o ta-bay-mash-ta)* |
| that restaurant | あのレストラン<br>**ano resutoran**<br>*(an-oh res-toh-run)* |
| in that restaurant | あのレストランで<br>**ano resutoran de**<br>*(an-oh res-toh-run day)* |
| yesterday | 昨日<br>**kinō**<br>**Kee-noh** |
| yesterday, I ate | 昨日、食べました<br>**kinō, tabemashita**<br>*(kee-noh ta-bay-mash-ta)* |
| Yesterday, I ate ramen in that restaurant with Mrs Suzuki. | 昨日、鈴木さんとあのレストランでラーメンを食べました。<br>**Kinō, Suzuki san to ano resutoran de rāmen o tabemashita.**<br>*(kee-noh su-zoo-kee sun to an-oh res-toh-run day ra-men o ta-bay-mash-ta)* |
| yesterday afternoon (literally "yesterday's afternoon") | 昨日の午後<br>**kinō no gogo**<br>*(kee-noh noh goh-goh)* |

| | |
|---|---|
| Yesterday afternoon, I went to Tokyo with Mrs Suzuki. | 昨日の午後、鈴木さんと東京に行きました。<br>**Kinō no gogo, Suzuki san to Tōkyō ni ikimashita.**<br>(kee-noh noh goh-goh su-zoo-kee sun to toh-kee-oh nee ik-ee-mash-ta) |
| to that restaurant | あのレストランに<br>**ano resutoran ni**<br>(an-oh res-toh-run nee) |
| yesterday evening / last night (literally "yesterday's evening") | 昨日の晩<br>**kinō no ban**<br>(kee-noh noh ban) |
| Yesterday evening, I went to that restaurant with Ms Tanaka. | 昨日の晩、田中さんとあのレストランに行きました。<br>**Kinō no ban, Tanaka san to ano resutoran ni ikimashita.**<br>(kee-noh noh ban ta-na-ka sun to res-toh-run nee ik-ee-mash-ta) |
| tempura | 天ぷら<br>**tenpura**<br>(ten-poo-ra) |
| she ate | 食べました<br>**tabemashita**<br>(ta-bay-mash-ta) |
| She ate tempura. | 天ぷらを食べました。<br>**Tenpura o tabemashita.**<br>(ten-poo-ra o ta-bay-mash-ta) |
| She ate tempura in the restaurant. | レストランで天ぷらを食べました。<br>**Resutoran de tenpura o tabemashita.**<br>(res-toh-run day ten-poo-ra o ta-bay-mash-ta) |
| She ate tempura in that restaurant. | あのレストランで天ぷらを食べました。<br>**Ano resutoran de tenpura o tabemashita.**<br>(an-oh res-toh-run day ten-poo-ra o ta-bay-mash-ta) |

| | |
|---|---|
| udon | うどん<br>**udon**<br>(oo-don) |
| he ate | 食べました<br>**tabemashita.**<br>(ta-bay-mash-ta) |
| He ate udon. | うどんを食べました。<br>**Udon o tabemashita.**<br>(oo-don o ta-bay-mash-ta) |
| He ate udon in the department store. | デパートでうどんを食べました。<br>**Depāto de udon o tabemashita.**<br>(day-par-toh day oo-don o ta-bay-mash-ta) |
| He ate udon in that department store. | あのデパートでうどんを食べました。<br>**Ano depāto de udon o tabemashita.**<br>(an-oh day-par-toh day oo-don o ta-bay-mash-ta) |
| Yesterday afternoon, he ate udon in that department store with Mr Tanaka. | 昨日の午後、田中さんとあのデパートでうどんを食べました。<br>**Kinō no gogo, Tanaka san to ano depāto de udon o tabemashita.**<br>(kee-noh noh goh-goh ta-na-ka sun to an-oh day-par-toh day oo-don o ta-bay-mash-ta) |
| we ate | 食べました<br>**tabemashita**<br>(ta-bay-mash-ta) |
| We ate udon. | うどんを食べました。<br>**Udon o tabemashita.**<br>(oo-don o ta-bay-mash-ta) |
| We ate udon last night. | 昨日の晩、うどんを食べました。<br>**Kinō no ban, udon o tabemashita.**<br>(kee-noh noh ban oo-don o ta-bay-mash-ta) |
| Okinawa | 沖縄<br>**Okinawa**<br>(ok-ee-now-a) |

| | |
|---|---|
| We ate udon in Okinawa last night. | 昨日の晩、沖縄でうどんを食べました。<br>**Kinō no ban, Okinawa de udon o tabemashita.**<br>*(kee-noh noh ban ok-ee-now-a day oo-don o ta-bay-mash-ta)* |
| she went | 行きました<br>**ikimashita**<br>*(ik-ee-mash-ta)* |
| he went | 行きました<br>**ikimashita**<br>*(ik-ee-mash-ta)* |
| we went | 行きました<br>**ikimashita**<br>*(ik-ee-mash-ta)* |
| We went to that restaurant yesterday afternoon. | 昨日の午後、あのレストランに行きました。<br>**Kinō no gogo, ano resutoran ni ikimashita.**<br>*(kee-noh noh goh-goh an-oh res-toh-run nee ik-ee-mash-ta)* |
| Hokkaido | 北海道<br>**Hokkaidō**<br>*(ho-kai-doh)* |
| We went to Hokkaido yesterday. | 昨日、北海道に行きました。<br>**Kinō, Hokkaidō ni ikimashita.**<br>*(kee-noh ho-kai-doh nee ik-ee-mash-ta.)* |
| Sapporo | 札幌<br>**Sapporo**<br>*(sa-po-roh)* |
| We ate in Sapporo. | 札幌で食べました。<br>**Sapporo de tabemashita.**<br>*(sa-po-roh day ta-bay-mash-ta)* |
| miso ramen | みそラーメン<br>**miso rāmen**<br>*(mee-soh ra-men)* |

| | |
|---|---|
| We ate miso ramen in Sapporo. | 札幌でみそラーメンを食べました。<br>**Sapporo de miso rāmen o tabemashita.**<br>(sa-po-roh day mee-soh ra-men o ta-bay-mash-ta) |
| We went to Hokkaido yesterday. We ate miso ramen in Sapporo. | 昨日、北海道に行きました。札幌でみそラーメンを食べました。<br>**Kinō, Hokkaidō ni ikimashita. Sapporo de miso rāmen o tabemashita.**<br>(kee-noh ho-kai-doh nee ik-ee-mash-ta. sa-po-roh day mee-soh ra-men o ta-bay-mash-ta) |
| it is | です<br>**desu**<br>(dess) |
| It's miso ramen. | みそラーメンです。<br>**Miso rāmen desu.**<br>(mee-soh ra-men dess) |
| It's a department store. | デパートです。<br>**Depāto desu.**<br>(day-par-toh dess) |
| was delicious | おいしかった<br>**Oishikatta**<br>(oy-sh-ka-ta) |
| It was delicious! | おいしかったです。<br>**Oishikatta desu!**<br>(oy-sh-ka-ta dess) |
| Yesterday afternoon, I ate miso ramen in Sapporo. It was delicious! | 昨日の午後、札幌でみそラーメンを食べました。おいしかったです。<br>**Kinō no gogo, Sapporo de miso rāmen o tabemashita. Oishikatta desu!**<br>(kee-noh noh goh-goh, sa-po-roh day mee-soh ra-men o ta-bay-mash-ta. oy-sh-ka-ta dess) |

| | |
|---|---|
| Yesterday, we went to Hokkaido. We ate miso ramen in Sapporo. It was delicious. | 昨日、北海道に行きました。札幌でみそラーメンを食べました。おいしかったです。<br>**Kinō, Hokkaido ni ikimashita. Sapporo de miso rāmen o tabemashita. Oishikatta desu!**<br>*(kee-noh, ho-kai-doh nee ik-ee-mash-ta. sa-po-roh day mee-soh ra-men o ta-bay-mash-ta. oy-sh-ka-ta dess)* |
| they went | 行きました<br>**ikimashita**<br>*(ik-ee-mash-ta)* |
| to Kyoto | 京都に<br>**Kyōto ni**<br>*(kee-oh-toh nee)* |
| They went to Kyoto. | 京都に行きました。<br>**Kyōto ni ikimashita.**<br>*(kee-oh-toh nee ik-ee-mash-ta)* |
| with me | 私と<br>**watashi to**<br>*(wa-ta-sh to)* |
| They went to Kyoto with me. | 私と京都に行きました。<br>**Watashi to Kyōto ni ikimashita.**<br>*(wa-ta-sh to kee-oh-toh nee ik-ee-mash-ta)* |
| last week | 先週<br>**sen shū**<br>*(sen shoo)* |
| Last week, they went to Kyoto with me. | 先週、私と京都に行きました。<br>**Sen shū, watashi to Kyōto ni ikimashita.**<br>*(sen shoo, wa-ta-sh to kee-oh-toh nee ik-ee-mash-ta)* |
| was interesting | 面白かった<br>**omoshirokatta**<br>*(om-osh-ee-ro-ka-ta)* |

| | |
|---|---|
| It was interesting! | 面白かったです！<br>**Omoshirokatta desu!**<br>(om-osh-ee-ro-ka-ta dess) |
| Last week, we went to Kyoto with Mrs Tanaka. It was interesting. | 先週、田中さんと京都に行きました。面白かったです。<br>**Sen shū, Tanaka san to Kyōto ni ikimashita. Omoshirokatta desu.**<br>(sen shoo, ta-na-ka sun to kee-oh-toh nee ik-ee-mash-ta. om-osh-ee-ro-ka-ta dess) |
| was beautiful | 美しかった<br>**utsukushikatta**<br>(oo-tsoo-koo-shee-ka-ta) |
| It was beautiful! | 美しかったです！<br>**Utsukushikatta desu!**<br>(oo-tsoo-koo-shee-ka-ta dess) |
| Last week, we went to Okinawa with Mrs Tanaka. It was beautiful. | 先週、田中さんと沖縄に行きました。美しかったです！<br>**Sen shū, Tanaka san to Okinawa ni ikimashita. Utsukushikatta desu!**<br>(sen shoo, ta-na-ka sun to ok-ee-now-a nee ik-ee-mash-ta. oo-tsoo-koo-shee-ka-ta dess) |

Well, that's it, you're done with Chapter Two! Remember, don't try to hold on to or remember anything you've learned here. Everything you learn in earlier chapters will be brought back up and reinforced in later chapters. You don't need to do anything or make any effort to memorise anything. The book has been organised in such a way that it will do that for you. So, off you go now and have a rest please!

## Between Chapters Tip 2!

## Stop while you're still enjoying it!

Arnold Schwarzenegger once said that the key to his body-building success was that he stopped his workout each day just *before* it started to get boring. On the few occasions that he went past that point, he found it incredibly hard to return to the gym again the next day – and he *loved* working out.

So, as you will almost certainly recall, Tip 1 suggested that you should study every day – which you definitely should do if you can. But that doesn't mean that you should overdo it. So, if you're not really in the mood, just do 5 minutes. If you are in the mood though, don't push yourself too hard. Stop before you get to the point where it doesn't feel fun any longer. Best to leave yourself feeling hungry for more rather than bloated and fed up!

# CHAPTER 3

I made a hotel reservation
online last night —
we're going to go to Kyoto!

## I made a hotel reservation online last night — we're going to go to Kyoto!

"I made a hotel reservation online last night." That sentence doesn't seem especially complicated in English and yet, even if you've studied Japanese before, you might well find it impossible to know where to begin in order to say this. By the end of this chapter, however, you will have learned how to build this sentence, plus a great deal more besides!

## Let's begin!

Once again, how would you say "I went"?

行きました
**ikimashita**
(ik-ee-mash-ta)

And how would you say "I ate":

食べました
**tabemashita**
(ta-bay-mash-ta)

"I did" or "I played" in Japanese is:

しました
**shimashita**
(shee-mash-ta)

How do you think you'd say "he did" / "he played"?

しました
**shimashita**
(shee-mash-ta)

How about "she played"?

しました
**shimashita**
(shee-mash-ta)

And "we played"?

しました
**shimashita**
(shee-mash-ta)

What about "they played"?

しました
**shimashita**
(shee-mash-ta)

"Basketball" in Japanese is:

バスケットボール
**basuketobōru**
(bask-et-oh-bor-oo)

Now again, what was "I played"?

しました
**shimashita**
(shee-mash-ta)

And what was "basketball"?

バスケットボール
**basuketobōru**
(bask-et-oh-bor-oo)

Now, if you want to say "I played basketball", you will follow the word "basketball" with an "o" just like you have so far been doing with food words, such as "ramen" or "sushi".

So, let's do that now. Say "I played basketball" – literally you'll say "basketball o I played":

バスケットボールをしました。
**Basuketobōru o shimashita.**
(bask-et-oh-bor-oo o shee-mash-ta)

Now, you may be wondering, why am I adding an "o" after "basketball"? I mean, we did it with food words but why are we doing it with "basketball"?

Well, just as "o" makes it clear to a Japanese listener that the food that the "o" goes after is the thing that's being eaten, so putting an "o" after a sport lets a Japanese listener know that it is *that* sport which is being played. Again, it's like a finger pointing back at the sport, saying "this is the thing I'm referring to, the thing that I've been playing". So, this "o" is actually really quite useful in Japanese – it has allowed us to make it clear what it is we've eaten and what it is we've played. I wonder what else it might let us do later on...

Anyway, for the moment, remind me, what is "she played"?

しました
**shimashita**
(shee-mash-ta)

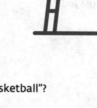

And what is "basketball"?

バスケットボール
**basuketobōru**
(bask-et-oh-bor-oo)

And, how would you say "she played basketball"?

バスケットボールをしました。
**Basuketobōru o shimashita.**
(bask-et-oh-bor-oo o shee-mash-ta)

What about "she played basketball in Sapporo"?

札幌でバスケットボールをしました。
**Sapporo de basuketobōru o shimashita.**
(sa-po-roh day bask-et-oh-bor-oo o shee-mash-ta)

And "she played basketball in Sapporo yesterday"?

昨日、札幌でバスケットボールをしました。
**Kinō, Sapporo de basuketobōru o shimashita.**
(kee-noh sa-po-roh day bask-et-oh-bor-oo o shee-mash-ta)

Asking a question in Japanese is extremely easy. All you need to do is to add a spoken question mark to the end of the sentence. The spoken question mark in Japanese is the word:

か
**ka**
(ka)

Now again, how would you say "she played"?

しました
**shimashita**
(shee-mash-ta)

And "she played basketball"?

バスケットボールをしました。
**Basuketobōru o shimashita.**
(bask-et-oh-bor-oo o shee-mash-ta)

And what is the spoken question mark?

か
**ka**
(ka)

Now, to ask "did she play basketball?" you'll simply say "she played basketball ka?" Do that now:

バスケットをしましたか。
**Basuketobōru o shimashita ka?**
(bask-et-oh-bor-oo o shee-mash-ta ka)

How would you say "did he play basketball?"

バスケットボールをしましたか。
**Basuketobōru o shimashita ka?**
(bask-et-oh-bor-oo o shee-mash-ta ka)

And "did he play basketball yesterday?"

昨日、バスケットボールをしましたか。
**Kinō, basuketobōru o shimashita ka?**
(kee-noh bask-et-oh-bor-oo o shee-mash-ta ka)

What was "last week"?

先週
**sen shū**
(sen shoo)

And so how would you say "did he play basketball last week?"

先週、バスケットボールをしましたか。
**Sen shū, basuketobōru o shimashita ka?**
(sen shoo bask-et-oh-bor-oo o shee-mash-ta ka)

"Tennis" in Japanese is:

テニス
**tenisu**
(ten-ee-soo)

So how would you say "did he play tennis last week?"

先週、テニスをしましたか。
**Sen shū, tenisu o shimashita ka?**
(sen shoo ten-ee-soo o shee-mash-ta ka)

Now, just on its own again, what is "I played" / "he played" / "she played" /
"we played" / "they played"?

しました
**shimashita**
(shee-mash-ta)

"You played" is also:

しました
**shimashita**
(shee-mash-ta)

So how would you say "you played tennis"?

テニスをしました。
**Tenisu o shimashita.**
(ten-ee-soo o shee-mash-ta)

What about "you played tennis last week"?

先週、テニスをしました。
**Sen shū, tenisu o shimashita.**
(sen shoo ten-ee-soo o shee-mash-ta)

Turn that into a question now and ask "did you play tennis last week?"

先週、テニスをしましたか。
**Sen shū, tenisu o shimashita ka?**
(sen shoo ten-ee-soo o shee-mash-ta ka)

And how would you say "did you play tennis with Mr Suzuki last week?"

先週、鈴木さんとテニスをしましたか。
**Sen shū, Suzuki san to tenisu o shimashita ka?**
(sen shoo su-zoo-kee sun to ten-ee-soo o shee-mash-ta ka)

What is "with me"?

私と
**watashi to**
(wa-tash to)

And again, what is "basketball"?

バスケットボール
**basuketobōru**
(bask-et-oh-bor-oo)

So how would you say "she played basketball with me last week"?

先週、私とテニスをしました。
**Sen shū, watashi to basuketobōru o shimashita.**
(sen shoo wa-tash to bask-et-oh-bor-oo o shee-mash-ta)

And "he played tennis with me yesterday"?

昨日、私とテニスをしました。
**Kinō, watashi to tenisu o shimashita.**
(*kee-noh wa-tash to ten-ee-soo o shee-mash-ta*)

Now once again, what is "I went"?

行きました
**ikimashita**
(*ik-ee-mash-ta*)

And how would you say "I went to the department store"?

デパートに行きました。
**Depāto ni ikimashita.**
(*day-par-toh nee ik-ee-mash-ta*)

"Hotel" or "the hotel" or "a hotel" in Japanese is:

ホテル
**hoteru**
(*hoh-te-roo*)

So how would you say "I went to the hotel"?

ホテルに行きました。
**Hoteru ni ikimashita.**
(*hoh-te-roo nee ik-ee-mash-ta*)

And again, what is "with me"?

私と
**Watashi to**
(*wa-tash to*)

And what is "last night" or "yesterday evening"?

昨日の晩
**kinō no ban**
(*kee-noh noh ban*)

So how would you say "they went to the hotel with me last night"?

昨日の晩、私とホテルに行きました。
**Kinō no ban, watashi to hoteru ni ikimashita.**
(kee-noh noh ban wa-tash to hoh-te-roo nee ik-ee-mash-ta)

What is "yesterday afternoon"?

昨日の午後
**kinō no gogo**
(kee-noh noh goh-goh)

Now that literally means "yesterday's afternoon". Given that's the case, which part of "kinō no gogo" represents the 's?

の
**no**
(noh)

Now again, what is "hotel" / "a hotel" / "the hotel"?

ホテル
**hoteru**
(hoh-te-roo)

So how would you say "the hotel's"?

ホテルの
**hoteru no**
(hoh-te-roo noh)

"Reservation" in Japanese is.

予約
**yoyaku**
(yoh-ya-koo)

If you want to say "a hotel reservation" you'll literally say "a hotel's reservation".

So, first of all what is "hotel's"?

ホテルの
**hoteru no**
(hoh-te-roo noh)

And as I've just told you, "reservation" in Japanese is:

予約
**yoyaku**
(yoh-ya-koo)

So how would you say "a hotel reservation" literally "hotel's reservation"?

ホテルの予約
**hoteru no yoyaku**
(hoh-te-roo noh yoh-ya-koo)

What is "I played" or "I did"?

しました
**shimashita**
(shee-mash-ta)

Now, in Japanese, you don't *make* a reservation, you *do* a reservation.

So once again, what is "a hotel reservation"?

ホテルの予約
**hoteru no yoyaku**
(hoh-te-roo noh yoh-ya-koo)

And so how would you say "I made a hotel reservation" – literally "I *did* a hotel's reservation"?

ホテルの予約をしました。
**Hoteru no yoyaku o shimashita.**
(hoh-te-roo noh yoh-ya-koo o shee-mash-ta)

Now, you may well be wondering, "why have we added an 'o' after 'hotel reservation'? I mean, we did it with food words and sports but why are we now also doing it with hotel reservations?" Well, it's because doing this makes it clear to a Japanese listener that the reservation is the thing that's been done.

So actually, the role of "o" is to tell the listener which word in the sentence is having something done to it. To show them what is on the receiving end of the action taking place in the sentence – to show them what it is that's been eaten or played with or done or whatever. Let's try to understand this better by building some more sentences with it!

What is "you did" / "you played"?

しました
**shimashita**
(shee-mash-ta)

So how would you say "you made a hotel reservation" / "you did a hotel's reservation"?

ホテルの予約をしました。
**Hoteru no yoyaku o shimashita.**
(hoh-te-roo noh yoh-ya-koo o shee-mash-ta)

What is the word that you add onto the end of a sentence to turn it into a question in Japanese?

か
**ka**
(ka)

So how would you say "did you make a hotel reservation?" – literally "you did a hotel's reservation ka?" How would you say that?

ホテルの予約をしましたか。
**Hoteru no yoyaku o shimashita ka?**
(hoh-te-roo noh yoh-ya-koo o shee-mash-ta ka)

And how would you ask "did they make a hotel reservation?"

ホテルの予約をしましたか。
**Hoteru no yoyaku o shimashita ka?**
(hoh-te-roo noh yoh-ya-koo o shee-mash-ta ka)

What is "department store" or "the department store"?

デパート
**depāto**
(day-par-toh)

And how would you say "in the department store"?

デパートで
**depāto de**
(day-par-toh day)

And which part of that means "in" or "in the"?

で
**de**
(day)

"The internet" in Japanese is:

インターネット
**intānetto**
(in-tah-ne-toh)

Now again what is "in" or "in the"?

で
**de**
(day)

And this word "de" can also mean "on" or "on the". So how would you say "on the internet"?

インターネットで
**intānetto de**
(in-tah-ne-toh day)

Notice how, just like when you used "de" to mean "in" with places, the "de" still goes after the word, not before. So, "in the department store" = "depāto de" and "on the internet" = "intānetto de". So, the "de" always comes after the word, not before it as in English.

Now again, what is "a hotel reservation"?

ホテルの予約
**hoteru no yoyaku**
(hoh-te-roo noh yoh-ya-koo)

And how would you say "I made a hotel reservation"?

ホテルの予約をしました。
**Hoteru no yoyaku o shimashita.**
(hoh-te-roo noh yoh-ya-koo o shee-mash-ta)

And what is "the internet"?

インターネット
**intānetto**
(in-tah-ne-toh)

And how would you say "on the internet"?

インターネットで
**intānetto de**
(in-tah-ne-toh day)

And so how would you say "I made a hotel reservation on the internet"?

インターネットでホテルの予約をしました。
**Intānetto de hoteru no yoyaku o shimashita.**
(in-tah-ne-toh day hoh-te-roo noh yoh-ya-koo o shee-mash-ta)

What is "last night"?

昨日の晩
**kinō no ban**
(kee-noh noh ban)

And so how would you say "I made a hotel reservation on the internet last night"?

昨日の晩、インターネットでホテルの予約をしました。
**Kinō no ban, intānetto de hoteru no yoyaku o shimashita.**
(kee-noh noh ban in-tah-ne-toh day hoh-te-roo noh yoh-ya-koo o shee-mash-ta)

What is "we went"?

行きました
**ikimashita**
(ik-ee-mash-ta)

"We go" or "we will go" or "we're going to go" in Japanese is:

行きます
**ikimasu**
(ik-ee-mass)

So, just the ending is different: "we went" ends in "mashita" but "we go" /
"we will go" / "we are going to go" ends in "masu".

So once again, what is "we went"?

行きました
**ikimashita**
(ik-*ee*-mash-ta)

But what is "we go", "we will go" or "we're going to go"?

行きます
**ikimasu**
(ik-*ee*-mass)

So how would you say "we're going to go to Hokkaido"?

北海道に行きます。
**Hokkaidō ni ikimasu.**
(ho-kai-doh *nee* ik-*ee*-mass)

How about "we're going to go to Okinawa"?

沖縄に行きます。
**Okinawa ni ikimasu.**
(ok-*ee*-now-a *nee* ik-*ee*-mass)

And "we're going to go to Kyoto"?

京都に行きます。
**Kyōto ni ikimasu.**
(kee-oh-toh *nee* ik-*ee*-mass)

"Bus" in Japanese is:

バス
**basu**
(bus-*oo*)

Now again, what is "in" or "in the" or "on" or "on the"?

で
**de**
(day)

And what was "bus"?

バス
**basu**
(bus-oo)

So how do you think you would say "on the bus"?

バスで
**basu de**
(bus-oo day)

And again, what is "we go", "we will go" or "we're going to go"?

行きます
**ikimasu**
(ik-ee-mass)

And "we will go to Kyoto"?

京都に行きます。
**Kyōto ni ikimasu.**
(kee-oh-toh nee ik-ee-mass)

And so how would you say "we will go to Kyoto on the bus" / "we will go to Kyoto by bus"?

バスで京都に行きます。
**Basu de Kyōto ni ikimasu.**
(bus-oo day kee-oh-toh nee ik-ee-mass)

How about "you will go to Kyoto by bus" / "you will go to Kyoto on the bus"?

バスで京都に行きます。
**Basu de Kyōto ni ikimasu.**
(bus-oo day kee-oh-toh nee ik-ee-mass)

Turn it into a question and ask "will you go to Kyoto by bus?"

バスで京都に行きますか。
**Basu de Kyōto ni ikimasu ka?**
(bus-oo day kee-oh-toh nee ik-ee-mass ka)

Now again, just on its own, what is "we go" / "we will go" / "we're going to go"?

行きます
**ikimasu**
(ik-ee-mass)

And so how would you say "we're going to go to Kyoto"?

京都に行きます。
**Kyōto ni ikimasu.**
(kee-oh-toh nee ik-ee-mass)

What was "I did"?

しました
**shimashita**
(shee-mash-ta)

And what is "a reservation"?

予約
**yoyaku**
(yoh-ya-koo)

And "a hotel reservation"?

ホテルの予約
**hoteru no yoyaku**
(hoh-te-roo noh yoh-ya-koo)

And so how would you say "I made a hotel reservation"?

ホテルの予約をしました。
**Hoteru no yoyaku o shimashita.**
(hoh-te-roo noh yoh-ya-koo o shee-mash-ta)

What is "the internet"?

インターネット
**intānetto**
(in-tah-ne-toh)

And how would you say "on the internet"?

インターネットで
**intānetto de**
(in-tah-ne-toh day)

And so how would you say "I made a hotel reservation online" literally "I did a hotel reservation on the internet"?

インターネットでホテルの予約をしました。
**Intānetto de hoteru no yoyaku o shimashita.**
(in-tah-ne-toh day hoh-te-roo noh yoh-ya-koo o shee-mash-ta)

How about "I made a hotel reservation online last night"?

昨日の晩、インターネットでホテルの予約をしました。
**Kinō no ban, intānetto de hoteru no yoyaku o shimashita.**
(kee-noh noh ban in-tah-ne-toh day hoh-te-roo noh yoh-ya-koo o shee-mash-ta)

And again, what is "we go", "we will go" or "we're going to go"?

行きます
**ikimasu**
(ik-ee-mass)

And so how would you say "we're going to go to Kyoto"?

京都に行きます。
**Kyōto ni ikimasu.**
(kee-oh-toh nee ik-ee-mass)

And now finally say "I made a hotel reservation online last night – we're going to go to Kyoto":

昨日の晩、インターネットでホテルの予約をしました。京都に行きます。
**Kinō no ban, intānetto de hoteru no yoyaku o shimashita – Kyōto ni ikimasu.**
(kee-noh noh ban in-tah-ne-toh day hoh-te-roo noh yoh-ya-koo o shee-mash-ta – kee-oh-toh nee ik-ee-mass)

How did you find that final, complex sentence? Even if you got it right, try constructing it a few more times, until you feel comfortable putting it together at speed. This will help you a great deal in the long term, as every time you practise building these longer sentences, the naturalness and fluidity of your spoken Japanese will improve, as will your confidence levels.

It's time again to add some new building blocks. Here they are:

So, you've got your new building blocks. Make as many sentences as you can!

---

1   Literally "today's afternoon".

You know what to do with the checklist now, so you don't need any reminding about that.

Do bear one thing in mind though. The checklists don't need to be done in one sitting. So, if you get through a page or two and feel that's enough then simply leave the rest until the next day. Always work at your own pace and don't do so much that you end up feeling overwhelmed. "Steady as she goes" should be your mantra!

|  |  |
|---|---|
| 東京<br>**Tōkyō**<br>(toh-kee-oh) | Tokyo |
| に<br>**ni**<br>(nee) | to |
| 東京に<br>**Tōkyō ni**<br>(toh-kee-oh nee) | to Tokyo |
| 行きました<br>**ikimashita**<br>(ik-ee-mash-ta) | I went |
| レストラン<br>**resutoran**<br>(res-toh-run) | restaurant / the restaurant / a restaurant |
| レストランに行きました。<br>**Resutoran ni ikimashita.**<br>(res-toh-run nee ik-ee-mash-ta) | I went to the restaurant. |
| と<br>**to**<br>(to) | with |
| Paulと<br>**Paul to**<br>(paul to) | with Paul |

|  |  |
|---|---|
| Paulとレストランに行きました。<br>**Paul to resutoran ni ikimashita.**<br>(paul to res-toh-run nee ik-ee-mash-ta) | I went to the restaurant with Paul. |
| Paulと東京に行きました。<br>**Paul to Tōkyō ni ikimashita.**<br>(paul to toh-kee-oh nee ik-ee-mash-ta) | I went to Tokyo with Paul. |
| デパート<br>**depāto**<br>(day-par-toh) | department store / the department store / a department store |
| さん<br>**san**<br>(sun) | Mr / Mrs / Ms |
| 鈴木さん<br>**Suzuki san**<br>(su-zoo-kee sun) | Mr Suzuki / Mrs Suzuki / Ms Suzuki |
| 鈴木さんとデパートに行きました。<br>**Suzuki san to depāto ni ikimashita.**<br>(su-zoo-kee sun to day-par-toh nee ik-ee-mash-ta) | I went to the department store with Ms Suzuki. |
| 食べました<br>**tabemashita**<br>(ta-bay-mash-ta) | I ate |
| Paulと食べました。<br>**Paul to tabemashita.**<br>(paul to ta-bay-mash-ta) | I ate with Paul. |
| すし<br>**sushi**<br>(sushi) | sushi |
| を<br>**o**<br>(o) | *The word that you put after the thing that's having something done to it.* |
| すしを食べました。<br>**Sushi o tabemashita.**<br>(sushi o ta-bay-mash-ta) | I ate sushi. |

| | |
|---|---|
| 鈴木さんとすしを食べました。<br>**Suzuki san to sushi o tabemashita.**<br>(su-zoo-kee sun to sushi o ta-bay-mash-ta) | I ate sushi with Mr Suzuki. |
| ラーメン<br>**rāmen**<br>(ra-men) | ramen / noodle soup |
| 鈴木さんとラーメンを食べました。<br>**Suzuki san to rāmen o tabemashita.**<br>(su-zoo-kee sun to ra-men o ta-bay-mash-ta) | I ate ramen with Mrs Suzuki. |
| で<br>**de**<br>(day) | in |
| レストランで<br>**resutoran de**<br>(res-toh-run day) | in the restaurant |
| 鈴木さんとレストランでラーメンを食べました。<br>**Suzuki san to resutoran de rāmen o tabemashita.**<br>(su-zoo-kee sun to res-toh-run day ra-men o ta-bay-mash-ta) | I ate ramen with Mrs Suzuki in the restaurant. |
| カツカレー<br>**katsu karē**<br>(kats ka-ray) | katsu curry |
| 田中さん<br>**Tanaka san**<br>(ta-na-ka sun) | Mr Tanaka / Mrs Tanaka / Ms Tanaka |
| 田中さんとレストランでカツカレーを食べました。<br>**Tanaka san to resutoran de katsu karē o tabemashita.**<br>(ta-na-ka sun to res-toh-run day kats ka-ray o ta-bay-mash-ta) | I ate katsu curry in the restaurant with Mr Tanaka. |

| | |
|---|---|
| デパートで<br>**depāto de**<br>(day-par-toh day) | in the department store |
| 田中さんとデパートでカツカレーを食べました。<br>**Tanaka san to depāto de katsu karē o tabemashita.**<br>(ta-na-ka sun to day-par-toh day kats ka-ray o ta-bay-mash-ta) | I ate katsu curry in the department store with Ms Tanaka. |
| あのデパート<br>**ano depāto**<br>(an-oh day-par-toh) | that department store |
| あのデパートで<br>**ano depāto de**<br>(an-oh day-par-toh day) | in that department store |
| 田中さんとあのデパートでカツカレーを食べました。<br>**Tanaka san to ano depāto de katsu karē o tabemashita.**<br>(ta-na-ka sun to an-oh day-par-toh day kats ka-ray o ta-bay-mash-ta) | I ate katsu curry in that department store with Ms Tanaka. |
| あのレストラン<br>**ano resutoran**<br>(an-oh res-toh-run) | that restaurant |
| あのレストランで<br>**ano resutoran de**<br>(an-oh res-toh-run day) | in that restaurant |
| 昨日<br>**kinō**<br>(kee-noh) | yesterday |
| 昨日、食べました<br>**kinō, tabemashita**<br>(kee-noh ta-bay-mash-ta) | yesterday, I ate |

| | |
|---|---|
| 昨日、鈴木さんとあのレストランでラーメンを食べました。<br>**Kinō, Suzuki san to ano resutoran de rāmen o tabemashita.**<br>(kee-noh su-zoo-kee sun to an-oh res-toh-run day ra-men o ta-bay-mash-ta) | Yesterday, I ate ramen in that restaurant with Mrs Suzuki. |
| 昨日の午後<br>**kinō no gogo**<br>(kee-noh noh goh-goh) | yesterday afternoon (literally "yesterday's afternoon") |
| 昨日の午後、鈴木さんと東京に行きました。<br>**Kinō no gogo, Suzuki san to Tōkyō ni ikimashita.**<br>(kee-noh noh goh-goh su-zoo-kee sun to toh-kee-oh nee ik-ee-mash-ta) | Yesterday afternoon, I went to Tokyo with Mrs Suzuki. |
| あのレストランに<br>**ano resutoran ni**<br>(an-oh res-toh-run nee) | to that restaurant |
| 昨日の晩<br>**kinō no ban**<br>(kee-noh noh ban) | yesterday evening / last night (literally "yesterday's evening") |
| 昨日の晩、田中さんとあのレストランに行きました。<br>**Kinō no ban, Tanaka san to ano resutoran ni ikimashita.**<br>(kee-noh noh ban ta-na-ka sun to res-toh-run nee ik-ee-mash-ta) | Yesterday evening, I went to that restaurant with Ms Tanaka. |
| 天ぷら<br>**tenpura**<br>(ten-poo-ra) | tempura |
| 食べました<br>**tabemashita**<br>(ta-bay-mash-ta) | she ate |
| 天ぷらを食べました。<br>**Tenpura o tabemashita.**<br>(ten-poo-ra o ta-bay-mash-ta) | She ate tempura. |

| | |
|---|---|
| レストランで天ぷらを食べました。<br>**Resutoran de tenpura o tabemashita.**<br>(res-toh-run day ten-poo-ra o ta-bay-mash-ta) | She ate tempura in the restaurant. |
| あのレストランで天ぷらを食べました。<br>**Ano resutoran de tenpura o tabemashita.**<br>(an-oh res-toh-run day ten-poo-ra o ta-bay-mash-ta) | She ate tempura in that restaurant. |
| うどん<br>**udon**<br>(oo-don) | udon |
| 食べました<br>**tabemashita.**<br>(ta-bay-mash-ta) | he ate |
| うどんを食べました。<br>**Udon o tabemashita.**<br>(oo-don o ta-bay-mash-ta) | He ate udon. |
| デパートでうどんを食べました。<br>**Depāto de udon o tabemashita.**<br>(day-par-toh day oo-don o ta-bay-mash-ta) | He ate udon in the department store. |
| あのデパートでうどんを食べました。<br>**Ano depāto de udon o tabemashita.**<br>(an-oh day-par-toh day oo-don o ta-bay-mash-ta) | He ate udon in that department store. |
| 昨日の午後、田中さんとあのデパートでうどんを食べました。<br>**Kinō no gogo, Tanaka san to ano depāto de udon o tabemashita.**<br>(kee-noh noh goh-goh ta-na-ka sun to an-oh day-par-toh day oo-don o ta-bay-mash-ta) | Yesterday afternoon, he ate udon in that department store with Mr Tanaka. |

| | |
|---|---|
| 食べました<br>**tabemashita**<br>(ta-bay-mash-ta) | we ate |
| うどんを食べました。<br>**Udon o tabemashita.**<br>(oo-don o ta-bay-mash-ta) | We ate udon. |
| 昨日の晩、うどんを食べました<br>**Kinō no ban, udon o tabemashita.**<br>(kee-noh noh ban oo-don o ta-bay-mash-ta) | We ate udon last night. |
| 沖縄<br>**Okinawa**<br>(ok-ee-now-a) | Okinawa |
| 昨日の晩、沖縄でうどんを食べました。<br>**Kinō no ban, Okinawa de udon o tabemashita.**<br>(kee-noh noh ban ok-ee-now-a day oo-don o ta-bay-mash-ta) | We ate udon in Okinawa last night. |
| 行きました<br>**ikimashita**<br>(ik-ee-mash-ta) | she went |
| 行きました<br>**ikimashita**<br>(ik-ee-mash-ta) | he went |
| 行きました<br>**ikimashita**<br>(ik-ee-mash-ta) | we went |
| 昨日の午後、あのレストランに行きました。<br>**Kinō no gogo, ano resutoran ni ikimashita.**<br>(kee-noh noh goh-goh an-oh res-toh-run nee ik-ee-mash-ta) | We went to that restaurant yesterday afternoon. |
| 北海道<br>**Hokkaidō**<br>(ho-kai-doh) | Hokkaido |

| | |
|---|---|
| 昨日、北海道に行きました。<br>**Kinō, Hokkaidō ni ikimashita.**<br>(kee-noh ho-kai-doh nee ik-ee-mash-ta.) | We went to Hokkaido yesterday. |
| 札幌<br>**Sapporo**<br>(sa-po-roh) | Sapporo |
| 札幌で食べました。<br>**Sapporo de tabemashita.**<br>(sa-po-roh day ta-bay-mash-ta) | We ate in Sapporo. |
| みそラーメン<br>**miso rāmen**<br>(mee-soh ra-men) | miso ramen |
| 札幌でみそラーメンを食べました。<br>**Sapporo de miso rāmen o tabemashita.**<br>(sa-po-roh day mee-soh ra-men o ta-bay-mash-ta) | We ate miso ramen in Sapporo. |
| 昨日、北海道に行きました。札幌でみそラーメンを食べました。<br>**Kinō, Hokkaidō ni ikimashita. Sapporo de miso rāmen o tabemashita.**<br>(kee-noh ho-kai-doh nee ik-ee-mash-ta. sa-po-roh day mee-soh ra-men o ta-bay-mash-ta) | We went to Hokkaido yesterday. We ate miso ramen in Sapporo. |
| です<br>**desu**<br>(dess) | it is |
| みそラーメンです。<br>**Miso rāmen desu.**<br>(mee-soh ra-men dess) | It's miso ramen. |
| デパートです。<br>**Depāto desu.**<br>(day-par-toh dess) | It's a department store. |

| | |
|---|---|
| おいしかった<br>**Oishikatta**<br>(oy-sh-ka-ta) | was delicious |
| おいしかったです！<br>**Oishikatta desu!**<br>(oy-sh-ka-ta dess) | It was delicious! |
| 昨日の午後、札幌でみそラーメンを食べました。おいしかったです。<br>**Kinō no gogo, Sapporo de miso rāmen o tabemashita. Oishikatta desu!**<br>(kee-noh noh goh-goh, sa-po-roh day mee-soh ra-men o ta-bay-mash-ta. oy-sh-ka-ta dess) | Yesterday afternoon, I ate miso ramen in Sapporo. It was delicious! |
| 昨日、北海道に行きました。札幌でみそラーメンを食べました。おいしかったです。<br>**Kinō, Hokkaidō ni ikimashita. Sapporo de miso rāmen o tabemashita. Oishikatta desu!**<br>(kee-noh, ho-kai-doh nee ik-ee-mash-ta. sa-po-roh day mee-soh ra-men o ta-bay-mash-ta. oy-sh-ka-ta dess) | Yesterday, we went to Hokkaido. We ate miso ramen in Sapporo. It was delicious. |
| 行きました<br>**ikimashita**<br>(ik-ee-mash-ta) | they went |
| 京都に<br>**Kyōto ni**<br>(kee-oh-toh nee) | to Kyoto |
| 京都に行きました。<br>**Kyōto ni ikimashita.**<br>(kee-oh-toh nee ik-ee-mash-ta) | They went to Kyoto. |
| 私と<br>**watashi to**<br>(wa-ta-sh to) | with me |

|  |  |
|---|---|
| 私と京都に行きました。<br>**Watashi to Kyōto ni ikimashita.**<br>(wa-ta-sh to kee-oh-toh nee ik-ee-mash-ta) | They went to Kyoto with me. |
| 先週<br>**sen shū**<br>(sen shoo) | last week |
| 先週、私と京都に行きました。<br>**Sen shū, watashi to Kyōto ni ikimashita.**<br>(sen shoo, wa-ta-sh to kee-oh-toh nee ik-ee-mash-ta) | Last week, they went to Kyoto with me. |
| 面白かった<br>**omoshirokatta**<br>(om-osh-ee-ro-ka-ta) | was interesting |
| 面白かったです。<br>**Omoshirokatta desu!**<br>(om-osh-ee-ro-ka-ta dess) | It was interesting! |
| 先週、田中さんと京都に行きました。面白かったです。<br>**Sen shū, Tanaka san to Kyōto ni ikimashita. Omoshirokatta desu.**<br>(sen shoo, ta-na-ka sun to kee-oh-toh nee ik-ee-mash-ta. om-osh-ee-ro-ka-ta dess) | Last week, we went to Kyoto with Mrs Tanaka. It was interesting. |
| 美しかった<br>**utsukushikatta**<br>(oo-tsoo-koo-shee-ka-ta) | was beautiful |
| 美しかったです！<br>**Utsukushikatta desu!**<br>(oo-tsoo-koo-shee-ka-ta dess) | It was beautiful! |
| 先週、田中さんと沖縄に行きました。美しかったです！<br>**Sen shū, Tanaka san to Okinawa ni ikimashita. Utsukushikatta desu!**<br>(sen shoo, ta-na-ka sun to ok-ee-now-a nee ik-ee-mash-ta. oo-tsoo-koo-shee-ka-ta dess) | Last week, we went to Okinawa with Mrs Tanaka. It was beautiful. |

| | |
|---|---|
| しました<br>**shimashita**<br>(shee-mash-ta) | I / he / she / they / we / you did<br>I / he / she / they / we / you played |
| バスケットボール<br>**basuketobōru**<br>(bask-et-oh-bor-oo) | basketball |
| バスケットボールをしました<br>**Basuketobōru o shimashita.**<br>(bask-et-oh-bor-oo o shee-mash-ta) | We played basketball. |
| 昨日、札幌でバスケットボール<br>をしました。<br>**Kinō, Sapporo de basuketobōru o**<br>**shimashita.**<br>(kee-noh sa-po-roh day bask-et-oh-<br>bor-oo o shee-mash-ta) | Yesterday, we played basketball in Sapporo. |
| か<br>**ka**<br>(ka) | *spoken question mark* |
| 先週、バスケットボールをしま<br>したか。<br>**Sen shū, basuketobōru o**<br>**shimashita ka?**<br>(sen shoo bask-et-oh-bor-oo o<br>shee-mash-ta ka) | Did you play basketball last week? |
| テニス<br>**tenisu**<br>(ten-ee-soo o) | tennis |
| 先週、テニスをしましたか。<br>**Sen shū, tenisu o shimashita ka?**<br>(sen shoo ten-ee-soo o shee-mash-<br>ta ka) | Did you play tennis last week? |
| 先週、鈴木さんとテニスをしま<br>したか。<br>**Sen shū, Suzuki san to tenisu o**<br>**shimashita ka?**<br>(sen shoo su zoo-kee sun to<br>ten-ee-soo o shee-mash-ta ka) | Last week, did you play tennis with Mr Suzuki? |

| | |
|---|---|
| ホテル<br>**hoteru**<br>(hoh-te-roo) | hotel / the hotel / a hotel |
| 昨日の晩、ホテルに行きました。<br>**Kinō no ban, hoteru ni ikimashita.**<br>(kee-noh noh ban hoh-te-roo nee ik-ee-mash-ta) | Last night, he went to the hotel. |
| 昨日の晩、私とホテルに行きました。<br>**Kinō no ban, watashi to hoteru ni ikimashita.**<br>(kee-noh noh ban wa-tash to hoh-te-roo nee ik-ee-mash-ta) | Last night, he went to the hotel with me. |
| の<br>**no**<br>(noh) | 's |
| 予約<br>**yoyaku**<br>(yoh-ya-koo) | reservation |
| ホテルの予約<br>**hoteru no yoyaku**<br>(hoh-te-roo noh yoh-ya-koo) | a hotel reservation / the hotel reservation |
| ホテルの予約をしました。<br>**Hoteru no yoyaku o shimashita.**<br>(hoh-te-roo noh yoh-ya-koo o shee-mash-ta) | I made a hotel reservation. |
| ホテルの予約をしましたか。<br>**Hoteru no yoyaku o shimashita ka?**<br>(hoh-te-roo noh yoh-ya-koo o shee-mash-ta ka) | Did you make a hotel reservation? |
| インターネット<br>**intānetto**<br>(in-tah-ne-toh) | internet / the internet |
| インターネットで<br>**intānetto de**<br>(in-tah-ne-toh day) | on the internet / online |

| | |
|---|---|
| インターネットでホテルの予約をしました。<br>**Intānetto de hoteru no yoyaku o shimashita.**<br>(in-tah-ne-toh day hoh-te-roo noh yoh-ya-koo o shee-mash-ta) | I made a hotel reservation online. |
| 昨日の晩、インターネットでホテルの予約をしました。<br>**Kinō no ban, intānetto de hoteru no yoyaku o shimashita.**<br>(kee-noh noh ban in-tah-ne-toh day hoh-te-roo noh yoh-ya-koo o shee-mash-ta) | Last night, I made a hotel reservation online. |
| 行きます<br>**ikimasu**<br>(ik-ee-mass) | I / he / she / they / we / you go / will go / are going to go |
| 京都<br>**Kyōto**<br>(kee-oh-toh) | Kyoto |
| 京都に行きます。<br>**Kyōto ni ikimasu.**<br>(kee-oh-toh nee ik-ee-mass) | I'm going to go to Kyoto. |
| 昨日の晩、インターネットでホテルの予約をしました。京都に行きます！<br>**Kinō no ban, intānetto de hoteru no yoyaku o shimashita – Kyōto ni ikimasu!**<br>(kee-noh noh ban in-tah-ne-toh day hoh-te-roo noh yoh-ya-koo o shee-mash-ta – kee-oh-toh nee ik-ee-mass) | Last night, I made a hotel reservation online – we're going to go to Kyoto! |
| 京都に行きますか。<br>**Kyōto ni ikimasu ka?**<br>(kee-oh-toh nee ik-ee-mass ka) | Are you going to go to Kyoto? |
| バス<br>**basu**<br>(bus-oo) | bus / the bus / a bus |
| バスで<br>**basu de**<br>(bus-oo day) | by bus |

| | |
|---|---|
| バスで京都に行きますか。<br>**Basu de Kyōto ni ikimasu ka?**<br>(bus-oo day kee-oh-toh nee ik-ee-mass ka) | Are you going to go to Kyoto by bus? |
| 今日<br>**kyō**<br>(kyoh) | today |
| 今日、バスで京都に行きます。<br>**Kyō, basu de Kyōto ni ikimasu.**<br>(kyoh bus-oo day kee-oh-toh nee ik-ee-mass) | I'm going to go to Kyoto by bus today. |
| タクシー<br>**takushii**<br>(tak-oo-shee) | taxi |
| タクシーで<br>**takushii de**<br>(tak-oo-shee day) | by taxi |
| 大阪<br>**Ōsaka**<br>(oh-sah-ka) | Osaka |
| 今日、タクシーで大阪に行きます。<br>**Kyō, takushii de Ōsaka ni ikimasu.**<br>(kyoh tak-oo-shee day oh-sah-ka nee ik-ee-mass) | Today, they're going to go to Osaka by taxi. |
| 今日の午後<br>**kyō no gogo**<br>(kyoh noh goh-goh) | this afternoon |
| 今日の午後、タクシーで大阪に行きますか。<br>**Kyō no gogo, takushii de Ōsaka ni ikimasu ka?**<br>(kyoh noh goh-goh tak-oo-shee day oh-sah-ka nee ik-ee-mass ka) | This afternoon, are you going to go to Osaka by taxi? |
| 電車<br>**densha**<br>(den-sha) | train |

| | |
|---|---|
| 電車で<br>**densha de**<br>(den-sha day) | by train |
| 広島に<br>**Hiroshima ni**<br>(hi-ro-shee-ma nee) | to Hiroshima |
| 電車で広島に行きますか。<br>**Densha de Hiroshima ni ikimasu ka?**<br>(den-sha day day hi-ro-shee-ma nee<br>ik-ee-mass ka) | Are you going to go to Hiroshima by train? |
| 今日、鈴木さんと電車で広島に<br>行きますか。<br>**Kyō, Suzuki san to densha de<br>Hiroshima ni ikimasu ka?**<br>(kyoh su-zoo-kee sun to den-sha day<br>day hi-ro-shee-ma nee ik-ee-mass ka) | Are you going to go to Hiroshima by train with Mrs Suzuki today? |

Now, time to do it the other way around!

| | |
|---|---|
| Tokyo | 東京<br>**Tōkyō**<br>(toh-kee-oh) |
| to | に<br>**ni**<br>(nee) |
| to Tokyo | 東京に<br>**Tōkyō ni**<br>(toh-kee-oh nee) |
| I went | 行きました<br>**ikimashita**<br>(ik-ee-mash-ta) |
| restaurant / the restaurant /<br>a restaurant | レストラン<br>**resutoran**<br>(res-toh-run) |
| I went to the restaurant. | レストランに行きました。<br>**Resutoran ni ikimashita.**<br>(res-toh-run nee ik-ee-mash-ta) |

| | |
|---|---|
| with | と<br>**to**<br>(to) |
| with Paul | Paulと<br>**Paul to**<br>(paul to) |
| I went to the restaurant with Paul. | Paulとレストランに行きました。<br>**Paul to resutoran ni ikimashita.**<br>(paul to res-toh-run nee ik-ee-mash-ta) |
| I went to Tokyo with Paul. | Paulと東京に行きました。<br>**Paul to Tōkyō ni ikimashita.**<br>(paul to toh-kee-oh nee ik-ee-mash-ta) |
| department store /<br>the department store /<br>a department store | デパート<br>**depāto**<br>(day-par-toh) |
| Mr / Mrs / Ms | さん<br>**san**<br>(sun) |
| Mr Suzuki / Mrs Suzuki / Ms Suzuki | 鈴木さん<br>**Suzuki san**<br>(su-zoo-kee sun) |
| I went to the department store with Ms Suzuki. | 鈴木さんとデパートに行きました。<br>**Suzuki san to depāto ni ikimashita.**<br>(su-zoo-kee sun to day-par-toh nee ik-ee-mash-ta) |
| I ate | 食べました<br>**tabemashita**<br>(ta-bay-mash-ta) |
| I ate with Paul. | Paulと食べました。<br>**Paul to tabemashita.**<br>(paul to ta-bay-mash-ta) |
| sushi | すし<br>**sushi**<br>(sushi) |

| | |
|---|---|
| *The word that you put after the thing that's been eaten.* | を<br>**o**<br>(o) |
| I ate sushi. | すしを食べました。<br>**Sushi o tabemashita.**<br>(sushi o ta-bay-mash-ta) |
| I ate sushi with Mr Suzuki. | 鈴木さんとすしを食べました。<br>**Suzuki san to sushi o tabemashita.**<br>(su-zoo-kee sun to sushi o ta-bay-mash-ta) |
| *ramen / noodle soup* | ラーメン<br>**rāmen**<br>(ra-men) |
| I ate ramen with Mrs Suzuki. | 鈴木さんとラーメンを食べました。<br>**Suzuki san to rāmen o tabemashita.**<br>(su-zoo-kee sun to ra-men o ta-bay-mash-ta) |
| *in* | で<br>**de**<br>(day) |
| in the restaurant | レストランで<br>**resutoran de**<br>(res-toh-run day) |
| I ate ramen with Mrs Suzuki in the restaurant. | 鈴木さんとレストランでラーメンを食べました。<br>**Suzuki san to resutoran de rāmen o tabemashita.**<br>(su-zoo-kee sun to res-toh-run day ra-men o ta-bay-mash-ta) |
| *katsu curry* | カツカレー<br>**katsu karē**<br>(kats ka-ray) |
| Mr Tanaka / Mrs Tanaka / Ms Tanaka | 田中さん<br>**Tanaka san**<br>(ta-na-ka sun) |

| | |
|---|---|
| I ate katsu curry in the restaurant with Mr Tanaka. | 田中さんとレストランでカツカレーを食べました。<br>**Tanaka san to resutoran de katsu karē o tabemashita.**<br>(ta-na-ka sun to res-toh-run day kats ka-ray o ta-bay-mash-ta) |
| in the department store | デパートで<br>**depāto de**<br>(day-par-toh day) |
| I ate katsu curry in the department store with Ms Tanaka. | 田中さんとデパートでカツカレーを食べました。<br>**Tanaka san to depāto de katsu karē o tabemashita.**<br>(ta-na-ka sun to day-par-toh day kats ka-ray o ta-bay-mash-ta) |
| that department store | あのデパート<br>**ano depāto**<br>(an-oh day-par-toh) |
| in that department store | あのデパートで<br>**ano depāto de**<br>(an-oh day-par-toh day) |
| I ate katsu curry in that department store with Ms Tanaka. | 田中さんとあのデパートでカツカレーを食べました。<br>**Tanaka san to ano depāto de katsu karē o tabemashita.**<br>(ta-na-ka sun to an-oh day-par-toh day kats ka-ray o ta-bay-mash-ta) |
| that restaurant | あのレストラン<br>**ano resutoran**<br>(an-oh res-toh-run) |
| in that restaurant | あのレストランで<br>**ano resutoran de**<br>(an-oh res-toh-run day) |
| yesterday | 昨日<br>**kinō**<br>**Kee-noh** |
| yesterday, I ate | 昨日、食べました<br>**kinō, tabemashita**<br>(kee-noh ta-bay-mash-ta) |

| | |
|---|---|
| Yesterday, I ate ramen in that restaurant with Mrs Suzuki. | 昨日、鈴木さんとあのデパートでラーメンを食べました。<br>**Kinō, Suzuki san to ano resutoran de rāmen o tabemashita.**<br>(kee-noh su-zoo-kee sun to an-oh res-toh-run day ra-men o ta-bay-mash-ta) |
| yesterday afternoon (literally "yesterday's afternoon") | 昨日の午後<br>**kinō no gogo**<br>(kee-noh noh goh-goh) |
| Yesterday afternoon, I went to Tokyo with Mrs Suzuki. | 昨日の午後、鈴木さんと東京に行きました。<br>**Kinō no gogo, Suzuki san to Tōkyō ni ikimashita.**<br>(kee-noh noh goh-goh su-zoo-kee sun to toh-kee-oh nee ik-ee-mash-ta) |
| to that restaurant | あのレストランに<br>**ano resutoran ni**<br>(an-oh res-toh-run nee) |
| yesterday evening / last night (literally "yesterday's evening") | 昨日の晩<br>**kinō no ban**<br>(kee-noh noh ban) |
| Yesterday evening, I went to that restaurant with Ms Tanaka. | 昨日の晩、田中さんとあのレストランに行きました。<br>**Kinō no ban, Tanaka san to ano resutoran ni ikimashita.**<br>(kee-noh noh ban ta-na-ka sun to res-toh-run nee ik-ee-mash-ta) |
| tempura | 天ぷら<br>**tenpura**<br>(ten-poo-ra) |
| she ate | 食べました<br>**tabemashita**<br>(ta-bay-mash-ta) |
| She ate tempura. | 天ぷらを食べました。<br>**Tenpura o tabemashita.**<br>(ten-poo-ra o ta-bay-mash-ta) |

| She ate tempura in the restaurant. | レストランで天ぷらを食べました。<br>**Resutoran de tenpura o tabemashita.**<br>(res-toh-run day ten-poo-ra o ta-bay-mash-ta) |
| --- | --- |
| She ate tempura in that restaurant. | あのレストランで天ぷらを食べました。<br>**Ano resutoran de tenpura o tabemashita.**<br>(an-oh res-toh-run day ten-poo-ra o ta-bay-mash-ta) |
| udon | うどん<br>**udon**<br>(oo-don) |
| he ate | 食べました<br>**tabemashita**<br>(ta-bay-mash-ta) |
| He ate udon. | うどんを食べました。<br>**Udon o tabemashita.**<br>(oo-don o ta-bay-mash-ta) |
| He ate udon in the department store. | デパートでうどんを食べました。<br>**Depāto de udon o tabemashita.**<br>(day-par-toh day oo-don o ta-bay-mash-ta) |
| He ate udon in that department store. | あのデパートでうどんを食べました。<br>**Ano depāto de udon o tabemashita.**<br>(an-oh day-par-toh day oo-don o ta-bay-mash-ta) |
| Yesterday afternoon, he ate udon in that department store with Mr Tanaka. | 昨日の午後、田中さんとあのデパートでうどんを食べました。<br>**Kinō no gogo, Tanaka san to ano depāto de udon o tabemashita.**<br>(kee-noh noh goh-goh ta-na-ka sun to an-oh day-par-toh day oo-don o ta-bay-mash-ta) |

| | |
|---|---|
| we ate | 食べました<br>**tabemashita**<br>(ta-bay-mash-ta) |
| We ate udon. | うどんを食べました。<br>**Udon o tabemashita.**<br>(oo-don o ta-bay-mash-ta) |
| We ate udon last night. | 昨日の晩、うどんを食べました。<br>**Kinō no ban, udon o tabemashita.**<br>(kee-noh noh ban oo-don o ta-bay-mash-ta) |
| Okinawa | 沖縄<br>**Okinawa**<br>(ok-ee-now-a) |
| We ate udon in Okinawa last night. | 昨日の晩、沖縄でうどんを食べました。<br>**Kinō no ban, Okinawa de udon o tabemashita.**<br>(kee-noh noh ban ok-ee-now-a day oo-don o ta-bay-mash-ta) |
| she went | 行きました<br>**ikimashita**<br>(ik-ee-mash-ta) |
| he went | 行きました<br>**ikimashita.**<br>(ik-ee-mash-ta) |
| we went | 行きました<br>**ikimashita**<br>(ik-ee-mash-ta) |
| We went to that restaurant yesterday afternoon. | 昨日の午後、あのレストランに行きました。<br>**Kinō no gogo, ano resutoran ni ikimashita.**<br>(kee-noh noh goh-goh an-oh res-toh-run nee ik-ee-mash-ta) |
| Hokkaido | 北海道<br>**Hokkaidō**<br>(ho-kai-doh) |

| | |
|---|---|
| We went to Hokkaido yesterday. | 昨日、北海道に行きました。<br>**Kinō, Hokkaidō ni ikimashita.**<br>(kee-noh ho-kai-doh nee ik-ee-<br>mash-ta.) |
| Sapporo | 札幌<br>**Sapporo**<br>(sa-po-roh) |
| We ate in Sapporo. | 札幌で食べました。<br>**Sapporo de tabemashita.**<br>(sa-po-roh day ta-bay-mash-ta) |
| miso ramen | みそラーメン<br>**miso rāmen**<br>(mee-soh ra-men) |
| We ate miso ramen in Sapporo. | 札幌でみそラーメンを食べました。<br>**Sapporo de miso rāmen o tabemashita.**<br>(sa-po-roh day mee-soh ra-men o ta-bay-mash-ta) |
| We went to Hokkaido yesterday.<br>We ate miso ramen in Sapporo. | 昨日、北海道に行きました。札幌でみそラーメンを食べました。<br>**Kinō, Hokkaidō ni ikimashita. Sapporo de miso rāmen o tabemashita.**<br>(kee-noh ho-kai-doh nee ik-ee-mash-ta. sa-po-roh day mee-soh ra-men o ta-bay-mash-ta) |
| it is | です<br>**desu**<br>(dess) |
| It's miso ramen. | みそラーメンです。<br>**Miso rāmen desu.**<br>(mee-soh ra-men dess) |
| It's a department store. | デパートです。<br>**Depāto desu.**<br>(day-par-toh dess) |

| | |
|---|---|
| was delicious | おいしかった<br>**Oishikatta**<br>(oy-sh-ka-ta) |
| It was delicious! | おいしかったです！<br>**Oishikatta desu!**<br>(oy-sh-ka-ta dess) |
| Yesterday afternoon, I ate miso ramen in Sapporo. It was delicious! | 昨日の午後、札幌でみそラーメンを食べました。おいしかったです。<br>**Kinō no gogo, Sapporo de miso rāmen o tabemashita. Oishikatta desu!**<br>(kee-noh noh goh-goh, sa-po-roh day mee-soh ra-men o ta-bay-mash-ta. oy-sh-ka-ta dess) |
| Yesterday, we went to Hokkaido. We ate miso ramen in Sapporo. It was delicious. | 昨日、北海道に行きました。札幌でみそラーメンを食べました。おいしかったです！<br>**Kinō, Hokkaidō ni ikimashita. Sapporo de miso rāmen o tabemashita. Oishikatta desu!**<br>(kee-noh, ho-kai-doh nee ik-ee-mash-ta. sa-po-roh day mee-soh ra-men o ta-bay-mash-ta. oy-sh-ka-ta dess) |
| they went | 行きました<br>**ikimashita**<br>(ik-ee-mash-ta) |
| to Kyoto | 京都に<br>**Kyōto ni**<br>(kee-oh-toh nee) |
| They went to Kyoto. | 京都に行きました。<br>**Kyōto ni ikimashita.**<br>(kee-oh-toh nee ik-ee-mash-ta) |
| with me | 私と<br>**watashi to**<br>(wa-ta-sh to) |

| | |
|---|---|
| They went to Kyoto with me. | 私と京都に行きました。<br>**Watashi to Kyōto ni ikimashita.**<br>(wa-ta-sh to kee-oh-toh nee ik-ee-mash-ta) |
| last week | 先週<br>**sen shū**<br>(sen shoo) |
| Last week, they went to Kyoto with me. | 先週、私と京都に行きました。<br>**Sen shū, watashi to Kyōto ni ikimashita.**<br>(sen shoo, wa-ta-sh to kee-oh-toh nee ik-ee-mash-ta) |
| was interesting | 面白かった<br>**omoshirokatta**<br>(om-osh-ee-ro-ka-ta) |
| It was interesting! | 面白かったです。<br>**Omoshirokatta desu!**<br>(om-osh-ee-ro-ka-ta dess) |
| Last week, we went to Kyoto with Mrs Tanaka. It was interesting. | 先週、田中さんと京都に行きました。面白かったです。<br>**Sen shū, Tanaka san to Kyōto ni ikimashita. Omoshirokatta desu.**<br>(sen shoo, ta-na-ka sun to kee-oh-toh nee ik-ee-mash-ta. om-osh-ee-ro-ka-ta dess) |
| was beautiful | 美しかった<br>**utsukushikatta**<br>(oo-tsoo-koo-shee-ka-ta) |
| It was beautiful! | 美しかったです！<br>**Utsukushikatta desu!**<br>(oo-tsoo-koo-shee-ka-ta dess) |
| Last week, we went to Okinawa with Mrs Tanaka. It was beautiful. | 先週、田中さんと沖縄に行きました。美しかったです。<br>**Sen shū, Tanaka san to Okinawa ni ikimashita. Utsukushikatta desu!**<br>(sen shoo, ta-na-ka sun to ok-ee-now-a nee ik-ee-mash-ta. oo-tsoo-koo-shee-ka-ta dess) |

| | |
|---|---|
| I / he / she / they / we / you did<br>I / he / she / they / we / you played | しました<br>**shimashita**<br>(shee-mash-ta) |
| basketball | バスケットボール<br>**basuketobōru**<br>(bask-et-oh-bor-oo) |
| We played basketball. | バスケットボールをしました。<br>**Basuketobōru o shimashita.**<br>(bask-et-oh-bor-oo o shee-mash-ta) |
| Yesterday, we played basketball in Sapporo. | 昨日、札幌でバスケットボールをしました。<br>**Kinō, Sapporo de basuketobōru o shimashita.**<br>(kee-noh sa-po-roh day bask-et-oh-bor-oo o shee-mash-ta) |
| *spoken question mark* | か<br>**ka**<br>(ka) |
| Did you play basketball last week? | 先週、バスケットボールをしましたか。<br>**Sen shū, basuketobōru o shimashita ka?**<br>(sen shoo bask-et-oh-bor-oo o shee-mash-ta ka) |
| tennis | テニス<br>**tenisu**<br>(ten-ee-soo) |
| Did you play tennis last week? | 先週、テニスをしましたか。<br>**Sen shū, tenisu o shimashita ka?**<br>(sen shoo ten-ee-soo o shee-mash-ta ka) |
| Last week, did you play tennis with Mr Suzuki? | 先週、鈴木さんとテニスをしましたか。<br>**Sen shū, Suzuki san to tenisu o shimashita ka?**<br>(sen shoo su-zoo-kee sun to ten-ee-soo o shee-mash-ta ka) |

| | |
|---|---|
| hotel / the hotel / a hotel | ホテル<br>**hoteru**<br>(hoh-te-roo) |
| Last night, he went to the hotel. | 昨日の晩、ホテルに行きました。<br>**Kinō no ban, hoteru ni ikimashita.**<br>(kee-noh noh ban hoh-te-roo nee ik-ee-mash-ta) |
| Last night, he went to the hotel with me. | 昨日の晩、私とホテルに行きました。<br>**Kinō no ban, watashi to hoteru ni ikimashita.**<br>(kee-noh noh ban wa-tash to hoh-te-roo nee ik-ee-mash-ta) |
| 's | の<br>**no**<br>(noh) |
| reservation | 予約<br>**yoyaku**<br>(yoh-ya-koo) |
| A hotel reservation / the hotel reservation | ホテルの予約<br>**hoteru no yoyaku**<br>(hoh-te-roo noh yoh-ya-koo) |
| I made a hotel reservation. | ホテルの予約をしました。<br>**Hoteru no yoyaku o shimashita.**<br>(hoh-te-roo noh yoh-ya-koo o shee-mash-ta) |
| Did you make a hotel reservation? | ホテルの予約をしましたか。<br>**Hoteru no yoyaku o shimashita ka?**<br>(hoh-te-roo noh yoh-ya-koo o shee-mash-ta ka) |
| internet / the internet | インターネット<br>**intānetto**<br>(in-tah-ne-toh) |
| on the internet / online | インターネットで<br>**intānetto de**<br>(in-tah-ne-toh day) |

| | |
|---|---|
| I made a hotel reservation online. | インターネットでホテルの予約をしました。<br>**Intānetto de hoteru no yoyaku o shimashita.**<br>(in-tah-ne-toh day hoh-te-roo noh yoh-ya-koo o shee-mash-ta) |
| Last night, I made a hotel reservation online. | 昨日の晩、インターネットでホテルの予約をしました。<br>**Kinō no ban, intānetto de hoteru no yoyaku o shimashita.**<br>(kee-noh noh ban in-tah-ne-toh day hoh-te-roo noh yoh-ya-koo o shee-mash-ta) |
| I / he / she / they / we / you go / will go / are going to go | 行きます<br>**ikimasu**<br>(ik-ee-mass) |
| Kyoto | 京都<br>**Kyōto**<br>(kee-oh-toh) |
| I'm going to go to Kyoto. | 京都に行きます。<br>**Kyōto ni ikimasu.**<br>(kee-oh-toh nee ik-ee-mass) |
| Last night, I made a hotel reservation online – we're going to go to Kyoto! | 昨日の晩、インターネットでホテルの予約をしました。京都に行きます！<br>**Kinō no ban, intānetto de hoteru no yoyaku o shimashita – Kyōto ni ikimasu!**<br>(kee-noh noh ban in-tah-ne-toh day hoh-te-roo noh yoh-ya-koo o shee-mash-ta – kee-oh-toh nee ik-ee-mass) |
| Are you going to go to Kyoto? | 京都に行きますか。<br>**Kyōto ni ikimasu ka?**<br>(kee-oh-toh nee ik-ee-mass ka) |
| bus / the bus / a bus | バス<br>**basu**<br>(bus-oo) |

| | |
|---|---|
| by bus | バスで<br>**basu de**<br>(bus-oo day) |
| Are you going to go to Kyoto by bus? | バスで京都に行きますか。<br>**Basu de Kyōto ni ikimasu ka?**<br>(bus-oo day kee-oh-toh nee ik-ee-mass ka) |
| today | 今日<br>**kyō**<br>(kyoh) |
| I'm going to go to Kyoto by bus today. | 今日、バスで京都に行きます。<br>**Kyō, basu de Kyōto ni ikimasu.**<br>(kyoh bus-oo day kee-oh-toh nee ik-ee-mass) |
| taxi | タクシー<br>**takushii**<br>(tak-oo-shee) |
| by taxi | タクシーで<br>**kakushii de**<br>(tak-oo-shee day) |
| Osaka | 大阪<br>**Ōsaka**<br>(oh-sah-ka) |
| Today, they're going to go to Osaka by taxi. | 今日、タクシーで大阪に行きます。<br>**Kyō, takushii de Ōsaka ni ikimasu.**<br>(kyoh tak-oo-shee day oh-sah-ka nee ik-ee-mass) |
| this afternoon | 今日の午後<br>**Kyō no gogo**<br>(kyoh noh goh-goh) |
| This afternoon, are you going to go to Osaka by taxi? | 今日の午後、タクシーで大阪に行きますか。<br>**Kyō no gogo, takushii de Ōsaka ni ikimasu ka?**<br>(kyoh noh goh-goh tak-oo-shee day oh-sah-ka nee ik-ee-mass ka) |

| train | 電車<br>**densha**<br>*(den-sha)* |
|---|---|
| **by train** | 電車で<br>**densha de**<br>*(den-sha day)* |
| **to Hiroshima** | 広島に<br>**Hiroshima ni**<br>*(hi-ro-shee-ma nee)* |
| **Are you going to go to Hiroshima by train?** | 電車で広島に行きますか。<br>**Densha de Hiroshima ni ikimasu ka?**<br>*(den-sha day day hi-ro-shee-ma nee ik-ee-mass ka)* |
| **Are you going to go to Hiroshima by train with Mrs Suzuki today?** | 今日、鈴木さんと電車で広島に行きますか。<br>**Kyō, Suzuki san to densha de Hiroshima ni ikimasu ka?**<br>*(kyoh su-zoo-kee sun to den-sha day day hi-ro-shee-ma nee ik-ee-mass ka)* |

well, that's it, you're done with Chapter 3!
Take a break!

## Use your "hidden moments"

A famous American linguist, Barry Farber, learned a great part of the languages he spoke during the "hidden moments" he found in everyday life. Such hidden moments might include the time he would spend waiting for a train to arrive or time spent waiting for the kids to come out of school or for the traffic to get moving in the morning. These hidden moments would otherwise have been useless and unimportant in his daily life but, for someone learning a language, they can be some of the most useful minutes of the day.

Breaking up your studies into lots of little bits like this can also be useful as a way to help stop them from feeling like a great effort or from becoming impractical when your life gets especially hectic.

So, keep this book in your pocket whenever you go out and then make use of such "hidden moments" whenever they come along!

# CHAPTER 4

It's good weather today, so I'm going to play football in the park with my family.

Another chapter, another complex – yet unquestionably learnable – sentence for us to tackle. Let's get to it!

**What is "I went"?**

行きました
**Ikimashita**
(ik-ee-mash-ta)

**And what is "I go" / "I will go" / "I'm going to go"?**

行きます
**Ikimasu**
(ik-ee-mass)

**And so how would you say "I'm going to go to Kyoto"?**

京都に行きます。
**Kyōto ni ikimasu.**
(kee-oh-toh ik-ee-mass)

**How about "I'm going to go to Tokyo"?**

東京に行きます。
**Tōkyō ni ikimasu.**
(toh-kee-oh nee ik-ee-mass)

**"Family" or "my family" in Japanese is:**

家族
**kazoku**
(ka-zok)

**So how do you think you'd say "with my family"?**

家族と
**kazoku to**
(ka-zok to)

And how would you say "I'm going to go to Tokyo with my family"?

家族と東京に行きます。
**Kazoku to Tōkyō ni ikimasu.**
(ka-zok to toh-kee-oh nee ik-ee-mass)

What is "this afternoon"?

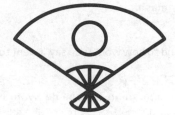

今日の午後
**kyō no gogo**
(kyoh noh goh-goh)

And so how would you say "I'm going to go to Hiroshima with my family this afternoon"?

今日の午後、家族と広島に行きます。
**Kyō no gogo, kazoku to Hiroshima ni ikimasu.**
(kyoh noh goh-goh ka-zok to hi-ro-shee-ma nee ik-ee-mass)

What is "by bus"?

バスで
**basu de**
(bus-oo day)

So how would you say "I'm going to go to Hiroshima with my family by bus this afternoon"?

今日の午後、家族とバスで広島に行きます。
**Kyō no gogo, kazoku to basu de Hiroshima ni ikimasu.**
(kyoh noh goh-goh ka-zok to bus-oo day hi-ro-shee-ma nee ik-ee-mass)

What is "by train"?

電車で
**densha de**
(den-sha day)

And again what is "yesterday afternoon"?

昨日の午後
**kinō no gogo**
(kee-noh noh goh-goh)

And what is "I went"?

行きました
**Ikimashita**
(ik-ee-mash-ta)

And so how would you say "I went to Kyoto by train yesterday afternoon"?

昨日の午後、電車で京都に行きました。
**Kinō no gogo, densha de Kyōto ni ikimashita.**
(kee-noh noh goh-goh den-sha day kee-oh-toh nee ik-ee-mash-ta)

What is "was beautiful"?

美しかった
**utsukushikatta**
(oo-tsoo-koo-shee-ka-ta)

And "it was beautiful"?

美しかったです！
**Utsukushikatta desu!**
(oo-tsoo-koo-shee-ka-ta dess)

So how would you say "I went to Kyoto yesterday afternoon by train.
It was beautiful!"?

昨日の午後、電車で京都に行きました。美しかったです！
**Kinō no gogo, densha de Kyōto ni ikimashita. Utsukushikatta desu!**
(kee-noh noh goh-goh den-sha day kee-oh-toh nee ik-ee-mash-ta.
oo-tsoo-koo-shee-ka-ta dess)

How would you say "it was interesting"?

面白かったです！
**Omoshirokatta desu!**
(om-osh-ee-ro-ka-ta dess)

And so how would you say "I went to Hiroshima yesterday afternoon.
It was interesting"?

昨日の午後、広島に行きました。面白かったです！
**Kinō no gogo, Hiroshima ni ikimashita. Omoshirokatta desu!**
(kee-noh noh goh-goh hi-ro-see-ma nee ik-ee-mash-ta. om-osh-ee-ro-ka-ta dess)

Again, what is "I go" / "I will go" / "I am going to go"?

行きます
**ikimasu**
(ik-*ee*-mass)

And how would you say "you go" / "you will go" / "you are going to go"?

行きます
**ikimasu**
(ik-*ee*-mass)

And how would you say "you are going to go to Osaka this afternoon"?

今日の午後、大阪に行きます。
**Kyō no gogo, Ōsaka ni ikimasu.**
(kyoh noh goh-goh oh-sah-ka nee ik-ee-mass)

Turn this into a question and ask "are you going to go to Osaka this afternoon?"

今日の午後、大阪に行きますか。
**Kyō no gogo, Ōsaka ni ikimasu ka?**
(kyoh noh goh-goh oh-sah-ka nee ik-ee-mass ka)

And now say "are you going to go to Osaka by train this afternoon?"

今日の午後、電車で大阪に行きますか。
**Kyō no gogo, densha de Ōsaka ni ikimasu ka?**
(kyoh noh goh-goh den-sha day oh-sah-ka nee ik-ee-mass ka)

What is "by bus"?

バスで
**basu de**
(bus-oo day)

And what is "by train"?

電車で
**densha de**
(den-sha day)

And what is "family" or "my family"?

家族
**kazoku**
(ka-zok)

And so how would you say "I'm going to go to Osaka by train with my family"?

家族と電車で大阪に行きます。
**Kazoku to densha de Ōsaka ni ikimasu.**
(ka-zok to den-sha day oh-sah-ka nee ik-ee-mass)

To say "your family" in Japanese, you'll say:

ご家族
**go Kazoku**
(go ka-zok)

So how would you say "with your family"?

ご家族と
**go Kazoku to**
(go ka-zok to)

Now again, what was "you go" / "you will go" / "you are going to go"?

行きます
**ikimasu**
(ik-ee-mass)

And so how would you ask "are you going to go to Osaka with your family?"

ご家族と大阪に行きますか。
**Go kazoku to Ōsaka ni ikimasu ka?**
(goh ka-zok to oh-sah-ka nee ik-ee-mass ka)

What about "are you going to go to Osaka with your family today?"

今日、ご家族と大阪に行きますか。
**Kyō, go kazoku to Ōsaka ni ikimasu ka?**
(kyoh goh ka-zok to oh-sah-ka nee ik-ee-mass ka)

Do you remember how to say "by taxi"?

タクシーで
**takushii de**
(tak-oo-shee day)

So how would you say "are you going to go to Osaka with your family by taxi today?"

今日、ご家族とタクシーで大阪に行きますか。
**Kyō, gokazoku to takushii de Ōsaka ni ikimasu ka?**
(kyoh goh ka-zok to tak-oo-shee day oh-sah-ka nee ik-ee-mass ka)

Now, once again, just on its own, what is "I go" / "I will go" / "I'm going to go"?

行きます
**ikimasu**
(ik-ee-mass)

And what is "I went"?

行きました
**ikimashita**
(ik-ee-mash-ta)

So, when we're talking about the present or future ("I go" / "I will go" / "I'm going to go") we put "masu" on the end and when we're talking about the past ("I went") we put "mashita" on the end.

What is "I ate"?

食べました
**tabemashita**
(ta-bay-mash-ta)

And so how would you say "I eat" / "I will eat" / "I'm going to eat"?

食べます
**tabemasu**
(tab-ay-mass)

And how would you say "I'm going to eat miso ramen"?

みそラーメンを食べます。
**Miso rāmen o tabemasu.**
(mee-soh ra-men o tab-ay-mass)

How about "she's going to eat miso ramen"?

みそラーメンを食べます。
**Miso rāmen o tabemasu.**
(mee-soh ra-men o tab-ay-mass)

What is "with me"?

私と
**watashi to**
(wa-tash to)

So how would you say "this afternoon, she's going to eat miso ramen with me"?

今日の午後、私とみそラーメンを食べます。
**Kyō no gogo, watashi to miso rāmen o tabemasu.**
(kyoh noh goh-goh wa-tash to mee-soh ra-men o tab-ay-mass)

"I drink" or "I will drink" or "I'm going to drink" in Japanese is:

飲みます
**nomimasu**
(no-mee-mass)

So how do you think you'd say "I drank"?

飲みました
**nomimashita**
(no-mee-mash-ta)

So, once again, we put "mashita" on the end when we're talking about the past and "masu" on the end when we're talking about the present or future.

What is "the restaurant"?

レストラン
**resutoran**
(res-toh-run)

And how would you say "in the restaurant"?

レストランで
**resutoran de**
(res-toh-run day)

And again "I drank" is:

飲みました
**nomimashita**
(no-mee-mash-ta)

So how would you say "I drank in the restaurant"?

レストランで飲みました。
**Resutoran de nomimashita.**
(res-toh-run day no-mee-mash-ta)

"Beer" in Japanese is:

ビール
**biiru**
(bee-roo)

So how would you say "I drank beer in the restaurant"?

レストランでビールを飲みました。
**Resutoran de biiru o nomimashita.**
(res-toh-run day bee-roo o no-mee-mash-ta)

Notice how we've placed an "o" after the word for beer to make it clear to the person you're talking to that it's the beer that's been drunk. We do this because "o" is there to let people know which thing is having something done to it, to let people know which thing has been played with, eaten, drunk or whatever.

What is "the hotel"?

ホテル
**hoteru**
(hoh-te-roo)

Can you work out how to say "the hotel restaurant" / "the hotel's restaurant"?

ホテルのレストラン
**hoteru no resutoran**
(hoh-te-roo noh res-toh-run)

And so how would you say "I drank beer in the hotel restaurant"?

ホテルのレストランでビールを飲みました。
**Hoteru no resutoran de biiru o nomimashita.**
(hoh-te-roo noh res-toh-run day bee-roo o no-mee-mash-ta)

"The bar" in Japanese is:

バー
**bā**
(bar)

So how would you say "in the bar"?

バーで
**bā de**
(bar-day)

And how would you say "I drank beer in the bar today"?

今日、バーでビールを飲みました。
**Kyō, bā de biiru o nomimashita.**
(kyoh bar day bee-roo o no-mee-mash-ta)

How do you think you would say "the hotel bar" / "the hotel's bar"?

ホテルのバー
**hoteru no bā**
(hoh-te-roo noh bar)

And so how would you say "I drank beer in the hotel bar today"?

今日、ホテルのバーでビールを飲みました。
**Kyō, hoteru no bā de biiru o nomimashita.**
(kyoh hoh-te-roo no bar day bee-roo o no-mee-mash-ta)

Turn that into a question and ask "did you drink beer in the hotel bar today?"

今日、ホテルのバーでビールを飲みましたか。
**Kyō, hoteru no bā de biiru o nomimashita ka?**
(kyoh bar day bee-roo o no-mee-mash-ta ka)

How about "did you drink beer with Paul in the hotel bar today?

今日、ポールとホテルのバーでビールを飲みましたか。
**Kyō, Paul to hoteru no bā de biiru o nomimashita ka?**
(kyoh paul to hoh-te-roo no bar day bee-roo o no-mee-mash-ta ka)

Again, what is "family" or "my family"?

家族
**kazoku**
(ka-zok)

So how would you say "I ate katsu curry in the hotel restaurant with my family today"?

今日、家族とホテルのレストランでカツカレーを食べました。
**Kyō, kazoku to hoteru no resutoran de katsu karē o tabemashita.**
(kyoh ka-zok to hoteru no res-to-run day kats ka-ray o ta-bay-mash-ta)

Now just on its own again, what is "I ate"?

食べました
**tabemashita**
(ta-bay-mash-ta)

And what is "I eat" / "I will eat" / "I'm going to eat"?

食べます
**tabemasu**
(tab-ay-mass)

What is "I went"?

行きました
**ikimashita**
(ik-ee-mash-ta)

And what is "I go" / "I will go" / "I'm going to go"?

行きます
**ikimasu**
(ik-ee-mass)

What is "I drank"?

飲みました
**nomimashita**
(no-mee-mash-ta)

And what is "in the bar"?

バーで
**bā de**
(bar day)

And what is "beer"?

ビール
**biiru**
(bee-roo)

And so how would you say "did you drink beer in the bar this afternoon?"

今日の午後、バーでビールを飲みましたか。
**Kyō no gogo, bā de biiru o nomimashita ka?**
(kyoh noh goh-goh bar day bee-roo o no-mee-mash-ta ka)

If "I drank" is "nomimashita", what would "I drink" / "I will drink" / "I'm going to drink" be?

飲みます
**nomimasu**
(no-mee-mass)

So, once again, we put "mashita" on the end when we're talking about the past and "masu" on the end when we're talking about the present or future.

How would you say "I'm going to drink beer with Mr Tanaka in the bar this afternoon"?

今日の午後、田中さんとバーでビールを飲みます。
**Kyō no gogo, Tanaka san to bā de biiru o nomimasu.**
(kyoh noh goh-goh ta-na-ka sun to bar day bee-roo o nom-ee-mass)

What was "I played" / "I did"?

しました
**shimashita**
(shee-mash-ta)

So what would be "I do" / "I play" / "I will do" / "I will play" / "I'm going to do" / "I'm going to play"?

します
**shimasu**
(shee-mass)

What is "basketball"?

バスケットボール
**basukettobōru**
(bask-et-oh-bor-oo)

And again what is "family" or "my family"?

家族
**kazoku**
(ka-zok)

So how would you say "I'm going to play basketball with my family this afternoon"?

今日の午後、家族とバスケットボールをします。
**Kyō no gogo, kazoku to basukettobōru o shimasu.**
(kyo noh goh-goh ka-zok to bask-et-oh-bor-oo o shee-mass)

"The park" in Japanese is:

公園
**kōen**
(koh-en)

So how would you say "in the park"?

公園で
**kōen de**
(koh-en day)

And how would you say "I'm going to play basketball in the park"?

公園でバスケットボールをします。
**Kōen de basukettobōru o shimasu.**
(ko-en day bask-et-oh-bor-oo o shee-mass)

How about "I'm going to play basketball in the park with my family this afternoon"?

今日の午後、家族と公園でバスケットボールをします。
**Kyō no gogo, kazoku to kōen de basukettobōru o shimasu.**
(kyo noh goh-goh ka-zok to ko-en day bask-et-oh-bor-oo o shee-mass)

What is "tennis"?

テニス
**tenisu**
(ten-ee-soo)

And do you remember how to say "your family"?

ご家族
**go kazoku**
(goh ka-zok)

And so how would you say "are you going to play tennis in the park with your family this afternoon?"

今日の午後、ご家族と公園でテニスをしますか。
**Kyō no gogo, go kazoku to kōen de tenisu o shimasu ka?**
(kyo noh goh-goh go ka-zok to ko-en day te-ni-soo o o shee-mass ka)

"Football" or "soccer" in Japanese is:

サッカー
**sakkā**
(sa-kaa)

So how would you say "I'm going to play football / soccer"?

サッカーをします。
**Sakkā o shimasu.**
(sa-kaa o shee-mass)

How about "you're going to play football / soccer"?

サッカーをします。
**Sakkā o shimasu.**
(sa-kaa o shee-mass)

And how about "are you going to play football in the park with your family today?"

今日、ご家族と公園でサッカーをしますか。
**Kyō, go kazoku to kōen de tenisu o shimasu ka?**
(kyo go ka-zok to ko-en day sa-kaa o shee-mass ka)

**What is "it is"?**

です
**desu**
(*dess*)

**So how would you say "it's a bar"?**

バーです。
**Bā desu.**
(*bar dess*)

**And how would you say "it's a park"?**

公園です。
**Kōen desu.**
(*koh-en dess*)

**How about "it's football"?**

サッカーです。
**Sakkā desu.**
(*sa-kaa dess*)

**And how about "it's beer"?**

ビールです。
**Biiru desu.**
(*bee-roo dess*)

If you want to say something is good in Japanese, the word you'll use for "good" is:

いい
**ii**
(*ee-ee*)

**So how would you say "it is good"?**

いいです
**ii desu**
(*ee-ee dess*)

Turn that into a question and ask "is it good?"

いいですか。
**Ii desu ka?**
(*ee-ee dess ka*)

"The weather" in Japanese is:

天気
**tenki**
(*ten-kee*)

Now again, how would you say "it is good"?

いいです
**ii desu**
(*ee-ee dess*)

And what was "weather"?

天気
**tenki**
(*ten-kee*)

Now, if you want to say "the weather is good" in Japanese, you'll literally say "the weather ga it is good." I'll explain why the "ga" is there in a moment but first of all, remind me again, what is "good"?

いい
**ii**
(*ee-ee*)

And what is "it is good"?

いいです
**ii desu**
(*ee-ee dess*)

And do you remember how to say "weather" / "the weather"?

天気
**tenki**
(*ten-kee*)

And so now try to say "the weather is good" - literally "the weather ga it is good":

天気がいいです。
**Tenki ga ii desu.**
(ten-kee ga ee-ee dess)

So, that means "the weather is good". But why did we need the "ga" in there? Well, "ga" is something you'll come across frequently in Japanese. It can be used for many different things, such as to emphasise the thing you're talking about or to show that you've just noticed something. Here it's kind of doing both. It's emphasising the fact that what you're talking about is the weather but it's also making it sound like you've only just noticed that the weather is good. "Ga" is a very interesting and useful word in Japanese and it's one that's best to understand simply by using it and getting a "feel" for it. Let's start doing that now!

Once again, what is "good"?

いい
**ii**
(ee-ee)

And how would you say "it is good"?

いいです
**ii desu**
(ee-ee dess)

And what is "weather" or "the weather"?

天気
**tenki**
(ten-kee)

And again how would you say "the weather is good"?

天気がいいです。
**Tenki ga ii desu.**
(ten-kee ga ee-ee dess)

What is "soccer" or "football"?

サッカー
**sakkā**
(sa-kaa)

And how would you say "I'm going to play football"?

サッカーをします。
**Sakkā o shimasu.**
(sa-kaa o shee-mass)

And again how would you say "the weather is good"?

天気がいいです。
**Tenki ga ii desu.**
(ten-kee ga ee-ee dess)

And so how would you say "The weather's good. I'm going to play football."?

天気がいいです。サッカーをします。
**Tenki ga ii desu. Sakkā o shimasu.**
(ten-kee ga ee-ee dess. sa-kaa o shee-mass)

What is "family" / "my family"?

家族
**kazoku**
(ka-zok)

And what is "the park"?

公園
**kōen**
(koh-en)

And what would be "in the park"?

公園で
**kōen de**
(koh-en day)

And so how would you say "The weather is good. I'm going to play football in the park with my family"?

天気がいいです。家族と公園でサッカーをします。
**Tenki ga ii desu. Kazoku to kōen de sakkā o shimasu.**
(ten-kee ga ee-ee dess. ka-zok to ko-en day sa-kaa o shee-mass)

**156**

"So" in Japanese is:

から
**kara**
(ka-ra)

So how would you say "The weather's good, so..."?

天気いいですから…
**Tenki ga ii desu kara…**
(ten-kee ga ee-ee dess, ka-ra…)

And now say "The weather's good, so I'm going to play football in the park with my family".

天気がいいですから、家族と公園でサッカーをします。
**Tenki ga ii desu kara kazoku to kōen de sakka o shimasu.**
(ten-kee ga ee-ee dess, ka-ra ka-zok to ko-en day aa-ka o shee-mass)

Not a bad sentence at all! Why not have a rest before going on to the next section – perhaps you could go to the park and play football with your family! What's that? You'd prefer to drink beer in a bar by yourself? Shocking! You'll be sitting at home, watching sumo on TV next...

Okay. Building block time. Here they are:

As before, let's use the building blocks below to make as many sentences as we can. Make sure to use every word at least once and, preferably, several times!

## well, off you go then!

| | |
|---|---|
| 東京<br>**Tōkyō**<br>(toh-kee-oh) | Tokyo |
| に<br>**ni**<br>(nee) | to |
| 東京に<br>**Tōkyō ni**<br>(toh-kee-oh nee) | to Tokyo |
| 行きました<br>**ikimashita**<br>(ik-ee-mash-ta) | I went |
| 行きました<br>**resutoran**<br>(res-toh-run) | restaurant / the restaurant / a restaurant |
| レストランに行きました。<br>**Resutoran ni ikimashita.**<br>(res-toh-run nee ik-ee-mash-ta) | I went to the restaurant. |
| と<br>**to**<br>(to) | with |
| Paulと<br>**Paul to**<br>(paul to) | with Paul |
| Paulとレストランに行きました。<br>**Paul to resutoran ni ikimashita.**<br>(paul to res-toh-run nee ik-ee-mash-ta) | I went to the restaurant with Paul. |
| Paulと東京に行きました。<br>**Paul to Tōkyō ni ikimashita.**<br>(paul to toh-kee-oh nee ik-ee-mash-ta) | I went to Tokyo with Paul. |

| | |
|---|---|
| デパート<br>**depāto**<br>(day-par-toh) | *department store / the department store / a department store* |
| さん<br>**san**<br>(sun) | Mr / Mrs / Ms |
| 鈴木さん<br>**Suzuki san**<br>(su-zoo-kee sun) | Mr Suzuki / Mrs Suzuki / Ms Suzuki |
| 鈴木さんとデパートに行きました。<br>**Suzuki san to depāto ni ikimashita.**<br>(su-zoo-kee sun to day-par-toh nee ik-ee-mash-ta) | I went to the department store with Ms Suzuki. |
| 食べました<br>**tabemashita**<br>(ta-bay-mash-ta) | I ate |
| Paulと食べました。<br>**Paul to tabemashita.**<br>(paul to ta-bay-mash-ta) | I ate with Paul. |
| すし<br>**sushi**<br>(sushi) | sushi |
| を<br>**o**<br>(o) | *The word that you put after the thing that's been eaten.* |
| すしを食べました。<br>**Sushi o tabemashita.**<br>(sushi o ta-bay-mash-ta) | I ate sushi. |
| 鈴木さんとすしを食べました。<br>**Suzuki san to sushi o tabemashita.**<br>(su-zoo-kee sun to sushi o ta-bay-mash-ta) | I ate sushi with Mr Suzuki. |
| ラーメン<br>**rāmen**<br>(ra-men) | ramen / noodle soup |

| | |
|---|---|
| 鈴木さんとラーメンを食べました。<br>**Suzuki san to rāmen o tabemashita.**<br>(su-zoo-kee sun to ra-men o ta-bay-mash-ta) | I ate ramen with Mrs Suzuki. |
| で<br>**de**<br>(day) | in |
| レストランで<br>**resutoran de**<br>(res-toh-run day) | in the restaurant |
| 鈴木さんとレストランでラーメンを食べました。<br>**Suzuki san to resutoran de rāmen o tabemashita.**<br>(su-zoo-kee sun to res-toh-run day ra-men o ta-bay-mash-ta) | I ate ramen with Mrs Suzuki in the restaurant. |
| カツカレー<br>**katsu karē**<br>(kats ka-ray) | katsu curry |
| 田中さん<br>**Tanaka san**<br>(ta-na-ka sun) | Mr Tanaka / Mrs Tanaka / Ms Tanaka |
| 田中さんとレストランでカツカレーを食べました。<br>**Tanaka san to resutoran de katsu karē o tabemashita.**<br>(ta-na-ka sun to res-toh-run day kats ka-ray o ta-bay-mash-ta') | I ate katsu curry in the restaurant with Mr Tanaka. |
| デパートで<br>**depāto de**<br>(day-par-toh day) | in the department store |
| 田中さんとデパートでカツカレーを食べました。<br>**Tanaka san to depāto de katsu karē o tabemashita.**<br>(ta-na-ka sun to day-par-toh day kats ka-ray o ta-bay-mash-ta) | I ate katsu curry in the department store with Ms Tanaka. |

| | |
|---|---|
| あのデパート<br>**ano depāto**<br>(an-oh day-par-toh) | that department store |
| あのデパートで<br>**ano depāto de**<br>(an-oh day-par-toh day) | in that department store |
| 田中さんとあのデパートでカツ<br>カレーを食べました。<br>**Tanaka san to ano depāto de katsu karē o tabemashita.**<br>(ta-na-ka sun to an-oh day-par-toh day kats ka-ray o ta-bay-mash-ta) | I ate katsu curry in that department store with Ms Tanaka. |
| あのレストラン<br>**ano resutoran**<br>(an-oh res-toh-run) | that restaurant |
| あのレストランで<br>**ano resutoran de**<br>(an-oh res-toh-run day) | in that restaurant |
| 昨日<br>**kinō**<br>(kee-noh) | yesterday |
| 昨日、食べました<br>**kinō, tabemashita**<br>(kee-noh ta-bay-mash-ta) | yesterday, I ate |
| 昨日、鈴木さんとあのレストラ<br>ンでラーメンを食べました。<br>**Kinō, Suzuki san to ano resutoran de rāmen o tabemashita.**<br>(kee-noh su-zoo-kee sun to an-oh res-toh-run day ra-men o ta-bay-mash-ta) | Yesterday, I ate ramen in that restaurant with Mrs Suzuki. |
| 昨日の午後<br>**kinō no gogo**<br>(kee-noh noh goh-goh) | yesterday afternoon (literally "yesterday's afternoon") |

|  |  |
|---|---|
| 昨日の午後、鈴木さんと東京に行きました。<br>**Kinō no gogo, Suzuki san to Tōkyō ni ikimashita.**<br>(kee-noh noh goh-goh su-zoo-kee sun to toh-kee-oh nee ik-ee-mash-ta) | Yesterday afternoon, I went to Tokyo with Mrs Suzuki. |
| あのレストランに<br>**ano resutoran ni**<br>(an-oh res-toh-run nee) | to that restaurant |
| 昨日の晩<br>**kinō no ban**<br>(kee-noh noh ban) | yesterday evening / last night<br>(literally "yesterday's evening") |
| 昨日の晩、田中さんとあのレストランに行きました。<br>**Kinō no ban, Tanaka san to ano resutoran ni ikimashita.**<br>(kee-noh noh ban ta-na-ka sun to res-toh-run nee ik-ee-mash-ta) | Yesterday evening, I went to that restaurant with Ms Tanaka. |
| 天ぷら<br>**tenpura**<br>(ten-poo-ra) | tempura |
| 食べました<br>**tabemashita**<br>(ta-bay-mash-ta) | she ate |
| 天ぷらを食べました。<br>**Tenpura o tabemashita.**<br>(ten-poo-ra o ta-bay-mash-ta) | She ate tempura. |
| レストランで天ぷらを食べました。<br>**Resutoran de tenpura o tabemashita.**<br>(res-toh-run day ten-poo-ra o ta-bay-mash-ta) | She ate tempura in the restaurant. |
| あのレストランで天ぷらを食べました。<br>**Ano resutoran de tenpura o tabemashita.**<br>(an-oh res-toh-run day ten-poo-ra o ta-bay-mash-ta) | She ate tempura in that restaurant. |

| | |
|---|---|
| うどん<br>**udon**<br>(oo-don) | udon |
| 食べました<br>**tabemashita**<br>(ta-bay-mash-ta) | he ate |
| うどんを食べました。<br>**Udon o tabemashita.**<br>(oo-don o ta-bay-mash-ta) | He ate udon. |
| デパートでうどんを食べました。<br>**Depāto de udon o tabemashita.**<br>(day-par-toh day oo-don o ta-bay-mash-ta) | He ate udon in the department store. |
| あのデパートでうどんを食べました。<br>**Ano depāto de udon o tabemashita.**<br>(an-oh day-par-toh day oo-don o ta-bay-mash-ta) | He ate udon in that department store. |
| 昨日の午後、田中さんとあのデパートでうどんを食べました。<br>**Kinō no gogo, Tanaka san to ano depāto de udon o tabemashita.**<br>(kee-noh noh goh-goh ta-na-ka sun to an-oh day-par-toh day oo-don o ta-bay-mash-ta) | Yesterday afternoon, he ate udon in that department store with Mr Tanaka. |
| 食べました<br>**tabemashita**<br>(ta-bay-mash-ta) | we ate |
| うどんを食べました。<br>**Udon o tabemashita.**<br>(oo-don o ta-bay-mash-ta) | We ate udon. |
| 昨日の晩、うどんを食べました。<br>**Kinō no ban, udon o tabemashita.**<br>(kee-noh noh ban oo-don o ta-bay-mash-ta) | We ate udon last night. |
| 沖縄<br>**Okinawa**<br>(ok-ee-now-a) | Okinawa |

| | |
|---|---|
| 昨日の晩、沖縄でうどんを食べました。<br>**Kinō no ban, Okinawa de udon o tabemashita.**<br>(kee-noh noh ban ok-ee-now-a day oo-don o ta-bay-mash-ta) | We ate udon in Okinawa last night. |
| 行きました<br>**ikimashita**<br>(ik-ee-mash-ta) | she went |
| 行きました<br>**ikimashita**<br>(ik-ee-mash-ta) | he went |
| 行きました<br>**ikimashita**<br>(ik-ee-mash-ta) | we went |
| 昨日の午後、あのレストランに行きました。<br>**Kinō no gogo, ano resutoran ni ikimashita.**<br>(kee-noh noh goh-goh an-oh res-toh-run nee ik-ee-mash-ta) | We went to that restaurant yesterday afternoon. |
| 北海道<br>**Hokkaidō**<br>(ho-kai-doh) | Hokkaido |
| 昨日、北海道に行きました。<br>**Kinō, Hokkaidō ni ikimashita.**<br>(kee-noh ho-kai-doh nee ik-ee-mash-ta.) | We went to Hokkaido yesterday. |
| 札幌<br>**Sapporo**<br>(sa-po-roh) | Sapporo |
| 札幌で食べました。<br>**Sapporo de tabemashita.**<br>(sa-po-roh day ta-bay-mash-ta) | We ate in Sapporo. |
| みそラーメン<br>**miso rāmen**<br>(mee-soh ra-men) | miso ramen |

| | |
|---|---|
| 札幌でみそラーメンを食べました。<br>**Sapporo de miso rāmen o tabemashita.**<br>(sa-po-roh day mee-soh ra-men o ta-bay-mash-ta) | We ate miso ramen in Sapporo. |
| 昨日、北海道に行きました。札幌でみそラーメンを食べました。<br>**Kinō, Hokkaidō ni ikimashita. Sapporo de miso rāmen o tabemashita.**<br>(kee-noh ho-kai-doh nee ik-ee-mash-ta. sa-po-roh day mee-soh ra-men o ta-bay-mash-ta) | We went to Hokkaido yesterday. We ate miso ramen in Sapporo. |
| です<br>**desu**<br>(dess) | it is |
| みそラーメンです。<br>**Miso rāmen desu.**<br>(mee-soh ra-men dess) | It's miso ramen. |
| デパートです。<br>**Depāto desu.**<br>(day-par-toh dess) | It's a department store. |
| おいしかった<br>**Oishikatta**<br>(oy-sh-ka-ta) | was delicious |
| おいしかったです！<br>**Oishikatta desu!**<br>(oy-sh-ka-ta dess) | It was delicious! |
| 昨日の午後、札幌でみそラーメンを食べました。おいしかったです！<br>**Kinō no gogo, Sapporo de miso rāmen o tabemashita. Oishikatta desu!**<br>(kee-noh noh goh-goh, sa-po-roh day mee-soh ra-men o ta-bay-mash-ta. oy-sh-ka-ta dess) | Yesterday afternoon, I ate miso ramen in Sapporo. It was delicious! |

|  |  |
|---|---|
| 昨日、北海道に行きました。札幌でみそラーメンを食べました。おいしかったです！<br>**Kinō, Hokkaidō ni ikimashita. Sapporo de miso rāmen o tabemashita. Oishikatta desu!**<br>(kee-noh, ho-kai-doh nee ik-ee-mash-ta. sa-po-roh day mee-soh ra-men o ta-bay-mash-ta. oy-sh-ka-ta dess) | Yesterday, we went to Hokkaido. We ate miso ramen in Sapporo. It was delicious. |
| 行きました<br>**ikimashita**<br>(ik-ee-mash-ta) | they went |
| 京都に<br>**Kyōto ni**<br>(kee-oh-toh nee) | to Kyoto |
| 京都に行きました。<br>**Kyōto ni ikimashita.**<br>(kee-oh-toh nee ik-ee-mash-ta) | They went to Kyoto. |
| 私と<br>**watashi to**<br>(wa-ta-sh to) | with me |
| 私と京都に行きました。<br>**Watashi to Kyōto ni ikimashita.**<br>(wa-ta-sh to kee-oh-toh nee ik-ee-mash-ta) | They went to Kyoto with me. |
| 先週<br>**sen shū**<br>(sen shoo) | last week |
| 先週、私と京都に行きました。<br>**Sen shū, watashi to Kyōto ni ikimashita.**<br>(sen shoo, wa-ta-sh to kee-oh-toh nee ik-ee-mash-ta) | Last week, they went to Kyoto with me. |
| 面白かった<br>**omoshirokatta**<br>(om-osh-ee-ro-ka-ta) | was interesting |

|  |  |
|---|---|
| 面白かったです！<br>**Omoshirokatta desu!**<br>(om-osh-ee-ro-ka-ta dess) | It was interesting! |
| 先週、田中さんと京都に行きました。面白かったです！<br>**Sen shū, Tanaka san to Kyōto ni ikimashita. Omoshirokatta desu.**<br>(sen shoo, ta-na-ka sun to kee-oh-toh nee ik-ee-mash-ta. om-osh-ee-ro-ka-ta dess) | Last week, we went to Kyoto with Mrs Tanaka. It was interesting. |
| 美しかった<br>**utsukushikatta**<br>(oo-tsoo-koo-shee-ka-ta) | was beautiful |
| 美しかったです！<br>**Utsukushikatta desu!**<br>(oo-tsoo-koo-shee-ka-ta dess) | It was beautiful! |
| 先週、田中さんと沖縄に行きました。美しかったです！<br>**Sen shū, Tanaka san to Okinawa ni ikimashita. Utsukushikatta desu!**<br>(sen shoo, ta-na-ka sun to ok-ee-now-a nee ik-ee-mash-ta. oo-tsoo-koo-shee-ka-ta dess) | Last week, we went to Okinawa with Mrs Tanaka. It was beautiful. |
| しました<br>**shimashita**<br>(shee-mash-ta) | I / he / she / they / we / you did<br>I / he / she / they / we / you played |
| バスケットボール<br>**basuketobōru**<br>(bask-et-oh-bor-oo) | basketball |
| バスケットボールをしました。<br>**Basuketobōru o shimashita.**<br>(bask-et-oh-bor-oo o shee-mash-ta) | We played basketball. |
| 昨日、札幌でバスケットボールをしました。<br>**Kinō, Sapporo de basuketobōru o shimashita.**<br>(kee-noh sa-po-roh day bask-et-oh-bor-oo o shee-mash-ta) | Yesterday, we played basketball in Sapporo. |

| | |
|---|---|
| か<br>**ka**<br>(ka) | *spoken question mark* |
| 先週、バスケットボールをしましたか。<br>**Sen shū, basuketobōru o shimashita ka?**<br>(sen shoo bask-et-oh-bor-oo o shee-mash-ta ka) | Did you play basketball last week? |
| テニス<br>**tenisu**<br>(ten-ee-soo o) | tennis |
| 先週、テニスをしましたか。<br>**Sen shū, tenisu o shimashita ka?**<br>(sen shoo ten-ee-soo o shee-mash-ta ka) | Did you play tennis last week? |
| 先週、鈴木さんとテニスをしましたか。<br>**Sen shū, Suzuki san to tenisu o shimashita ka?**<br>(sen shoo su-zoo-kee sun to ten-ee-soo o shee-mash-ta ka) | Last week, did you play tennis with Mr Suzuki? |
| ホテル<br>**hoteru**<br>(hoh-te-roo) | hotel / the hotel / a hotel |
| 昨日の晩、ホテルに行きました。<br>**Kinō no ban, hoteru ni ikimashita.**<br>(kee-noh noh ban hoh-te-roo nee ik-ee-mash-ta) | Last night, he went to the hotel. |
| 昨日の晩、私とホテルに行きました。<br>**Kinō no ban, watashi to hoteru ni ikimashita.**<br>(kee-noh noh ban wa-tash to hoh-te-roo nee ik-ee-mash-ta) | Last night, he went to the hotel with me. |
| の<br>**no**<br>(noh) | 's |

| | |
|---|---|
| 予約<br>**yoyaku**<br>(yoh-ya-koo) | reservation |
| ホテルの予約<br>**hoteru no yoyaku**<br>(hoh-te-roo noh yoh-ya-koo) | a hotel reservation / the hotel reservation |
| ホテルの予約をしました。<br>**Hoteru no yoyaku o shimashita.**<br>(hoh-te-roo noh yoh-ya-koo o shee-mash-ta) | I made a hotel reservation. |
| ホテルの予約をしましたか。<br>**Hoteru no yoyaku o shimashita ka?**<br>(hoh-te-roo noh yoh-ya-koo o shee-mash-ta ka) | Did you make a hotel reservation? |
| インターネット<br>**intānetto**<br>(in-tah-ne-toh) | internet / the internet |
| インターネットで<br>**intānetto de**<br>(in-tah-ne-toh day) | on the internet / online |
| インターネットでホテルの予約をしました。<br>**Intānetto de hoteru no yoyaku o shimashita.**<br>(in-tah-ne-toh day hoh-te-roo noh yoh-ya-koo o shee-mash-ta) | I made a hotel reservation online. |
| 昨日の晩、インターネットでホテルの予約をしました。<br>**Kinō no ban, intānetto de hoteru no yoyaku o shimashita.**<br>(kee-noh noh ban in-tah-ne-toh day hoh-te-roo noh yoh-ya-koo o shee-mash-ta) | Last night, I made a hotel reservation online. |
| 行きます<br>**ikimasu**<br>(ik-ee-mass) | I / he / she / they / we / you go / will go / are going to go |

| | |
|---|---|
| 京都<br>**Kyōto**<br>(kee-oh-toh) | Kyoto |
| 京都に行きます。<br>**Kyōto ni ikimasu.**<br>(kee-oh-toh nee ik-ee-mass) | I'm going to go to Kyoto. |
| 昨日の晩、インターネットでホテルの予約をしました。京都に行きます。<br>**Kinō no ban, intānetto de hoteru no yoyaku o shimashita – Kyōto ni ikimasu!**<br>(kee-noh noh ban in-tah-ne-toh day hoh-te-roo noh yoh-ya-koo o shee-mash-ta – kee-oh-toh nee ik-ee-mass) | Last night, I made a hotel reservation online – we're going to go to Kyoto! |
| 京都に行きますか。<br>**Kyōto ni ikimasu ka?**<br>(kee-oh-toh nee ik-ee-mass ka) | Are you going to go to Kyoto? |
| バス<br>**basu**<br>(bus-oo) | bus / the bus / a bus |
| バスで<br>**basu de**<br>(bus-oo day) | by bus |
| バスで京都に行きますか。<br>**Basu de Kyōto ni ikimasu ka?**<br>(bus-oo day kee-oh-toh nee ik-ee-mass ka) | Are you going to go to Kyoto by bus? |
| 今日<br>**kyō**<br>(kyoh) | today |
| 今日、バスで京都に行きます。<br>**Kyō, basu de Kyōto ni ikimasu.**<br>(kyoh bus-oo day kee-oh-toh nee ik-ee-mass) | I'm going to go to Kyoto by bus today. |

| | |
|---|---|
| タクシー<br>**takushii**<br>(tak-oo-shee) | taxi |
| タクシーで<br>**takushii de**<br>(tak-oo-shee day) | by taxi |
| 大阪<br>**Ōsaka**<br>(oh-sah-ka) | Osaka |
| 今日、タクシーで大阪に行きます。<br>**Kyō, takushii de Ōsaka ni ikimasu.**<br>(kyoh tak-oo-shee day oh-sah-ka nee ik-ee-mass) | Today, they're going to go to Osaka by taxi. |
| 今日の午後<br>**kyō no gogo**<br>(kyoh noh goh-goh) | this afternoon |
| 今日の午後、タクシーで大阪に行きますか。<br>**Kyō no gogo, takushii de Ōsaka ni ikimasu ka?**<br>(kyoh noh goh-goh tak-oo-shee day oh-sah-ka nee ik-ee-mass ka) | This afternoon, are you going to go to Osaka by taxi? |
| 電車<br>**densha**<br>(den-sha) | train |
| 広島に<br>**Hiroshima ni**<br>(hi-ro-shee-ma nee) | to Hiroshima |
| 電車で広島に行きますか。<br>**Densha de Hiroshima ni ikimasu ka?**<br>(den-sha day day hi-ro-shee-ma nee ik-ee-mass ka) | Are you going to go to Hiroshima by train? |
| 今日、鈴木さんと電車で広島に行きますか。<br>**Kyō, Suzuki san to densha de Hiroshima ni ikimasu ka?**<br>(kyoh su-zoo-kee sun to den-sha day day hi-ro-shee-ma nee ik-ee-mass ka) | Are you going to go to Hiroshima by train with Mrs Suzuki today? |

| 家族<br>**kazoku**<br>(ka-zok) | family / the family / my family |
|---|---|
| 今日の午後、家族とバスで広島に行きます。<br>**Kyō no gogo, kazoku to basu de Hiroshima ni ikimasu.**<br>(kyoh noh goh-goh ka-zok to bus-oo day hi-ro-shee-ma nee ik-ee-mass) | I'm going to go to Hiroshima by bus with my family this afternoon. |
| ご家族<br>**go kazoku**<br>(goh ka-zok) | your family |
| 今日、ご家族とタクシーでデパートに行きますか。<br>**Kyō, go kazoku to takushii de depāto ni ikimasu ka?**<br>(kyoh goh ka-zok to tak-oo-shee day day-par-toh nee ik-ee-mass ka) | Are you going to go to the department store with your family by taxi today? |
| ビール<br>**biiru**<br>(bee-roo) | beer / the beer |
| ホテルのレストラン<br>**hoteru no resutoran**<br>(hoh-te-roo noh res-toh-run) | the hotel restaurant / the hotel's restaurant |
| ホテルのレストランでビールを飲みました。<br>**Hoteru no resutoran de biiru o nomimashita.**<br>(hoh-te-roo noh res-toh-run day bee-roo o no-mee-mash-ta) | I drank beer in the hotel restaurant. |
| バー<br>**bā**<br>(bar) | bar / the bar |
| バーでビールを飲みました。<br>**Bā de biiru o nomimashita.**<br>(bar day bee-roo o no-mee-mash-ta) | I drank beer in the bar. |

| | |
|---|---|
| ホテルのバー<br>**hoteru no bā**<br>(hoh-te-roo noh bar) | the hotel bar / the hotel's bar |
| 今日、田中さんとホテルのレストランでビールを飲みましたか。<br>**Kyō, Tanaka san to hoteru no bā de biiru o nomimashita ka?**<br>(kyoh ta-na-ka sun to hoh-te-roo no bar day bee-roo o no-mee-mash-ta ka) | Did you drink beer in the hotel bar with Mr Tanaka today? |
| 公園<br>**kōen**<br>(ko-en) | park / the park |
| サッカー<br>**sakkā**<br>(sa-kaa) | football / soccer |
| 今日の午後、ご家族と公園でサッカーをしますか。<br>**Kyō no gogo, go kazoku to kōen de sakkā o shimasu ka?**<br>(kyo noh goh-goh go ka-zok to ko-en day sa-kaa o shee-mass ka) | Are you going to play football in the park with your family this afternoon? |
| 天気<br>**tenki**<br>(ten-kee) | weather / the weather |
| が<br>**ga**<br>(ga) | *Word that helps add some emphasis to the word that it goes after; it can also make it clear that this is the subject you're talking about and it's also often used when someone has just noticed something.* |
| 天気がいいです。<br>**Tenki ga ii desu.**<br>(ten-kee ga ee-ee dess) | The weather is good. |
| から<br>**kara**<br>(ka-ra) | so |

|  |  |
|---|---|
| 天気がいいですから、家族と公園でサッカーをします。<br>**Tenki ga ii desu kara kazoku to kōen de sakkā o shimasu.**<br>(ten-kee ga ee-ee dess, ka-ra ka-zok to ko-en day saa-ka o shee-mass) | The weather is good so I'm going to play football in the park with my family. |
| 見ました<br>**mimashita**<br>(mee-mash-ta) | I / he / she / we / they / you watched |
| 相撲<br>**sumō**<br>(soo-moh) | sumo |
| テレビで<br>**terebi de**<br>(te-re-bee day) | on TV |
| 今朝<br>**kesa**<br>(ke-sa) | this morning |
| 今朝、テレビで相撲を見ました。<br>**Kesa, terebi de sumō o mimashita.**<br>(ke-sa te-re-bee day soo-moh o mee-mash-ta) | This morning, we watched sumo on TV. |
| アニメ<br>**anime**<br>(a-nee-may) | anime |
| 昨日の朝<br>**kinō no asa**<br>(kee noh noh a-sa) | yesterday morning |
| 昨日の朝、テレビでアニメを見ました。<br>**Kinō no asa, terebi de anime o mimashita.**<br>(kee-noh noh a-sa te-re-bee day a-nee-may o mee-mash-ta) | Yesterday morning, we watched an anime on TV. |

# Now, time to do it the other way around!

| Tokyo | 東京<br>**Tōkyō**<br>(toh-kee-oh) |
|---|---|
| to | に<br>**ni**<br>(nee) |
| to Tokyo | 東京に<br>**Tōkyō ni**<br>(toh-kee-oh nee) |
| I went | 行きました<br>**ikimashita**<br>(ik-ee-mash-ta) |
| restaurant / the restaurant /<br>a restaurant | レストラン<br>**resutoran**<br>(res-toh-run) |
| I went to the restaurant. | レストランに行きました。<br>**Resutoran ni ikimashita.**<br>(res-toh-run nee ik-ee-mash-ta) |
| with | と<br>**to**<br>(to) |
| with Paul | Paulと<br>**Paul to**<br>(paul to) |
| I went to the restaurant with Paul. | Paulとレストランに行きました。<br>**Paul to resutoran ni ikimashita.**<br>(paul to res-toh-run nee ik-ee-mash-ta) |
| I went to Tokyo with Paul. | Paulと東京に行きました。<br>**Paul to Tōkyō ni ikimashita.**<br>(paul to toh-kee-oh nee ik-ee-mash-ta) |
| department store / the<br>department store / a department<br>store | デパート<br>**depāto**<br>(day-par-toh) |

| | |
|---|---|
| Mr / Mrs / Ms | さん<br>**san**<br>(sun) |
| Mr Suzuki / Mrs Suzuki / Ms Suzuki | 鈴木さん<br>**Suzuki san**<br>(su-zoo-kee sun) |
| I went to the department store with Ms Suzuki. | 鈴木さんとデパートに行きました。<br>**Suzuki san to depāto ni ikimashita.**<br>(su-zoo-kee sun to day-par-toh nee ik-ee-mash-ta) |
| I ate | 食べました<br>**tabemashita**<br>(ta-bay-mash-ta) |
| I ate with Paul. | Paulと食べました。<br>**Paul to tabemashita.**<br>(paul to ta-bay-mash-ta) |
| sushi | すし<br>**sushi**<br>(sushi) |
| *The word that you put after the thing that's been eaten.* | を<br>**o**<br>(o) |
| I ate sushi. | すしを食べました。<br>**Sushi o tabemashita.**<br>(sushi o ta-bay-mash-ta) |
| I ate sushi with Mr Suzuki. | 鈴木さんとすしを食べました。<br>**Suzuki san to sushi o tabemashita.**<br>(su-zoo-kee sun to sushi o ta-bay-mash-ta) |
| ramen / noodle soup | ラーメン<br>**rāmen**<br>(ra-men) |

| | |
|---|---|
| I ate ramen with Mrs Suzuki. | 鈴木さんとラーメンを食べました。<br>Suzuki san to rāmen o tabemashita.<br>(su-zoo-kee sun to ra-men o ta-bay-mash-ta) |
| in | で<br>de<br>(day) |
| in the restaurant | レストランで<br>resutoran de<br>(res-toh-run day) |
| I ate ramen with Mrs Suzuki in the restaurant. | 鈴木さんとレストランでラーメンを食べました。<br>Suzuki san to resutoran de rāmen o tabemashita.<br>(su-zoo-kee sun to res-toh-run day ra-men o ta-bay-mash-ta) |
| katsu curry | カツカレー<br>katsu karē<br>(kats ka-ray) |
| Mr Tanaka / Mrs Tanaka / Ms Tanaka | 田中さん<br>Tanaka san<br>(ta-na-ka sun) |
| I ate katsu curry in the restaurant with Mr Tanaka. | 田中さんとレストランでカツカレーを食べました。<br>Tanaka san to resutoran de katsu karē o tabemashita.<br>(ta-na-ka sun to res-toh-run day kats ka-ray o ta-bay-mash-ta) |
| in the department store | デパートで<br>depāto de<br>(day-par-toh day) |

| | |
|---|---|
| I ate katsu curry in the department store with Ms Tanaka. | 田中さんとデパートでカツカレーを食べました。<br>**Tanaka san to depāto de katsu karē o tabemashita.**<br>(ta-na-ka sun to day-par-toh day kats ka-ray o ta-bay-mash-ta) |
| that department store | あのデパート<br>**ano depāto**<br>(an-oh day-par-toh) |
| in that department store | あのデパートで<br>**ano depāto de**<br>(an-oh day-par-toh day) |
| I ate katsu curry in that department store with Ms Tanaka. | 田中さんとあのデパートでカツカレーを食べました。<br>**Tanaka san to ano depāto de katsu karē o tabemashita.**<br>(ta-na-ka sun to an-oh day-par-toh day kats ka-ray o ta-bay-mash-ta) |
| that restaurant | あのレストラン<br>**ano resutoran**<br>(an-oh res-toh-run) |
| in that restaurant | あのレストランで<br>**ano resutoran de**<br>(an-oh res-toh-run day) |
| yesterday | 昨日<br>**kinō**<br>**Kee-noh** |
| yesterday, I ate | 昨日、食べました<br>**kinō, tabemashita**<br>(kee-noh ta-bay-mash-ta) |
| Yesterday, I ate ramen in that restaurant with Mrs Suzuki. | 昨日、鈴木さんとあのレストランでラーメンを食べました。<br>**Kinō, Suzuki san to ano resutoran de rāmen o tabemashita.**<br>(kee-noh su-zoo-kee sun to an-oh res-toh-run day ra-men o ta-bay-mash-ta) |

| | |
|---|---|
| yesterday afternoon (literally "yesterday's afternoon") | 昨日の午後<br>kinō no gogo<br>(kee-noh noh goh-goh) |
| Yesterday afternoon, I went to Tokyo with Mrs Suzuki. | 昨日の午後、鈴木さんと東京に行きました。<br>Kinō no gogo, Suzuki san to Tōkyō ni ikimashita.<br>(kee-noh noh goh-goh su-zoo-kee sun to toh-kee-oh nee ik-ee-mash-ta) |
| to that restaurant | あのレストランに<br>ano resutoran ni<br>(an-oh res-toh-run nee) |
| yesterday evening / last night (literally "yesterday's evening") | 昨日の晩<br>kinō no ban<br>(kee-noh noh ban) |
| Yesterday evening, I went to that restaurant with Ms Tanaka. | 昨日の晩、田中さんとあのレストランに行きました。<br>Kinō no ban, Tanaka san to ano resutoran ni ikimashita.<br>(kee-noh noh ban ta-na-ka sun to res-toh-run nee ik-ee-mash-ta) |
| tempura | 天ぷら<br>tenpura<br>(ten-poo-ra) |
| she ate | 食べました<br>tabemashita<br>(ta-bay-mash-ta) |
| She ate tempura. | 天ぷらを食べました。<br>Tenpura o tabemashita.<br>(ten-poo-ra o ta-bay-mash-ta) |
| She ate tempura in the restaurant. | レストランで天ぷらを食べました。<br>Resutoran de tenpura o tabemashita.<br>(res-toh-run day ten-poo-ra o ta-bay-mash-ta) |

| | |
|---|---|
| She ate tempura in that restaurant. | あのレストランで天ぷらを食べました。<br>**Ano resutoran de tenpura o tabemashita.**<br>*(an-oh res-toh-run day ten-poo-ra o ta-bay-mash-ta)* |
| udon | うどん<br>**udon**<br>*(oo-don)* |
| he ate | 食べました<br>**tabemashita.**<br>*(ta-bay-mash-ta)* |
| He ate udon. | うどんを食べました。<br>**Udon o tabemashita.**<br>*(oo-don o ta-bay-mash-ta)* |
| He ate udon in the department store. | デパートでうどんを食べました。<br>**Depāto de udon o tabemashita.**<br>*(day-par-toh day oo-don o ta-bay-mash-ta)* |
| He ate udon in that department store. | あのデパートでうどんを食べました。<br>**Ano depāto de udon o tabemashita.**<br>*(an-oh day-par-toh day oo-don o ta-bay-mash-ta)* |
| Yesterday afternoon, he ate udon in that department store with Mr Tanaka. | 昨日の午後、田中さんとあのデパートでうどんを食べました。<br>**Kinō no gogo, Tanaka san to ano depāto de udon o tabemashita.**<br>*(koo-noh noh goh-goh ta-na-ka sun to an-oh day-par-toh day oo-don o ta-bay-mash-ta)* |
| we ate | 食べました<br>**tabemashita**<br>*(ta-bay-mash-ta)* |
| We ate udon. | うどんを食べました。<br>**Udon o tabemashita.**<br>*(oo-don o ta-bay-mash-ta)* |

| | |
|---|---|
| We ate udon last night. | 昨日の晩、うどんを食べました。<br>**Kinō no ban, udon o tabemashita.**<br>(kee-noh noh ban oo-don o ta-bay-mash-ta) |
| Okinawa | 沖縄<br>**Okinawa**<br>(ok-ee-now-a) |
| We ate udon in Okinawa last night. | 昨日の晩、沖縄でうどんを食べました。<br>**Kinō no ban, Okinawa de udon o tabemashita.**<br>(kee-noh noh ban ok-ee-now-a day oo-don o ta-bay-mash-ta) |
| she went | 行きました<br>**ikimashita**<br>(ik-ee-mash-ta) |
| he went | 行きました<br>**ikimashita**<br>(ik-ee-mash-ta) |
| we went | 行きました<br>**ikimashita**<br>(ik-ee-mash-ta) |
| We went to that restaurant yesterday afternoon. | 昨日の午後、あのレストランに行きました。<br>**Kinō no gogo, ano resutoran ni ikimashita.**<br>(kee-noh noh goh-goh an-oh res-toh-run nee ik-ee-mash-ta) |
| Hokkaido | 北海道<br>**Hokkaidō**<br>(ho-kai-doh) |
| We went to Hokkaido yesterday. | 昨日、北海道に行きました。<br>**Kinō, Hokkaidō ni ikimashita.**<br>(kee-noh ho-kai-doh nee ik-ee-mash-ta.) |
| Sapporo | 札幌<br>**Sapporo**<br>(sa-po-roh) |

| | |
|---|---|
| We ate in Sapporo. | 札幌で食べました。<br>**Sapporo de tabemashita.**<br>(sa-po-roh day ta-bay-mash-ta) |
| miso ramen | みそラーメン<br>**miso rāmen**<br>(mee-soh ra-men) |
| We ate miso ramen in Sapporo. | 札幌でみそラーメンを食べました。<br>**Sapporo de miso rāmen o tabemashita.**<br>(sa-po-roh day mee-soh ra-men o ta-bay-mash-ta) |
| We went to Hokkaido yesterday.<br>We ate miso ramen in Sapporo. | 昨日、北海道に行きました。札幌でみそラーメンを食べました。<br>**Kinō, Hokkaidō ni ikimashita.**<br>**Sapporo de miso rāmen o tabemashita.**<br>(kee-noh ho-kai-doh nee ik-ee-mash-ta. sa-po-roh day mee-soh ra-men o ta-bay-mash-ta) |
| it is | です<br>**desu**<br>(dess) |
| It's miso ramen. | みそラーメンです。<br>**Miso rāmen desu.**<br>(mee-soh ra-men dess) |
| It's a department store. | デパートです。<br>**Depāto desu.**<br>(day-par toh dess) |
| was delicious | おいしかった<br>**Oishikatta**<br>(oy-sh-ka-ta) |
| It was delicious! | おいしかったです！<br>**Oishikatta desu!**<br>(oy-sh-ka-ta dess) |

| | |
|---|---|
| Yesterday afternoon, I ate miso ramen in Sapporo. It was delicious! | 昨日の午後、札幌でみそラーメンを食べました。おいしかったです！<br>**Kinō no gogo, Sapporo de miso rāmen o tabemashita. Oishikatta desu!**<br>(kee-noh noh goh-goh, sa-po-roh day mee-soh ra-men o ta-bay-mash-ta. oy-sh-ka-ta dess) |
| Yesterday, we went to Hokkaido. We ate miso ramen in Sapporo. It was delicious. | 昨日、北海道に行きました。札幌でみそラーメンを食べました。おいしかったです！<br>**Kinō, Hokkaidō ni ikimashita. Sapporo de miso rāmen o tabemashita. Oishikatta desu!**<br>(kee-noh, ho-kai-doh nee ik-ee-mash-ta. sa-po-roh day mee-soh ra-men o ta-bay-mash-ta. oy-sh-ka-ta dess) |
| they went | 行きました<br>**ikimashita**<br>(ik-ee-mash-ta) |
| to Kyoto | 京都に<br>**Kyōto ni**<br>(kee-oh-toh nee) |
| They went to Kyoto. | 京都に行きました。<br>**Kyōto ni ikimashita.**<br>(kee-oh-toh nee ik-ee-mash-ta) |
| with me | 私と<br>**watashi to**<br>(wa-ta-sh to) |
| They went to Kyoto with me. | 私と京都に行きました。<br>**Watashi to Kyōto ni ikimashita.**<br>(wa-ta-sh to kee-oh-toh nee ik-ee-mash-ta) |
| last week | 先週<br>**sen shū**<br>(sen shoo) |

| | |
|---|---|
| Last week, they went to Kyoto with me. | 先週、私と京都に行きました。<br>**Sen shū, watashi to Kyōto ni ikimashita.**<br>(sen shoo, wa-ta-sh to kee-oh-toh nee ik-ee-mash-ta) |
| was interesting | 面白かった<br>**omoshirokatta**<br>(om-osh-ee-ro-ka-ta) |
| It was interesting! | 面白かったです！<br>**Omoshirokatta desu!**<br>(om-osh-ee-ro-ka-ta dess) |
| Last week, we went to Kyoto with Mrs Tanaka. It was interesting. | 先週、田中さんと京都に行きました。面白かったです！<br>**Sen shū, Tanaka san to Kyōto ni ikimashita. Omoshirokatta desu.**<br>(sen shoo, ta-na-ka sun to kee-oh-toh nee ik-ee-mash-ta. om-osh-ee-ro-ka-ta dess) |
| was beautiful | 美しかった<br>**utsukushikatta**<br>(oo-tsoo-koo-shee-ka-ta) |
| It was beautiful! | 美しかったです！<br>**Utsukushikatta desu!**<br>(oo-tsoo-koo-shee-ka-ta dess) |
| Last week, we went to Okinawa with Mrs Tanaka. It was beautiful. | 先週、田中さんと沖縄に行きました。美しかったです！<br>**Sen shū, Tanaka san to Okinawa ni ikimashita. Utsukushikatta desu!**<br>(sen shoo, ta-na-ka sun to ok-ee-now-a nee ik-ee-mash-ta. oo-tsoo-koo-shee-ka-ta dess) |
| I / he / she / they / we / you did<br>I / he / she / they / we / you played | しました<br>**shimashita**<br>(shee-mash-ta) |
| basketball | バスケットボール<br>**basuketobōru**<br>(bask-et-oh-bor-oo) |

| | |
|---|---|
| We played basketball. | バスケットボールをしました。<br>**Basuketobōru o shimashita.**<br>(bask-et-oh-bor-oo o shee-mash-ta) |
| Yesterday, we played basketball in Sapporo. | 昨日、札幌でバスケットボールをしました。<br>**Kinō, Sapporo de basuketobōru o shimashita.**<br>(kee-noh sa-po-roh day bask-et-oh-bor-oo o shee-mash-ta) |
| spoken question mark | か<br>**ka**<br>(ka) |
| Did you play basketball last week? | 先週、バスケットボールをしましたか。<br>**Sen shū, basuketobōru o shimashita ka?**<br>(sen shoo bask-et-oh-bor-oo o shee-mash-ta ka) |
| tennis | テニス<br>**tenisu**<br>(ten-ee-soo o) |
| Did you play tennis last week? | 先週、テニスをしましたか。<br>**Sen shū, tenisu o shimashita ka?**<br>(sen shoo ten-ee-soo o shee-mash-ta ka) |
| Last week, did you play tennis with Mr Suzuki? | 先週、鈴木さんとテニスをしましたか。<br>**Sen shū, Suzuki san to tenisu o shimashita ka?**<br>(sen shoo su-zoo-kee sun to ten-ee-soo o shee-mash-ta ka) |
| hotel / the hotel / a hotel | ホテル<br>**hoteru**<br>(hoh-te-roo) |
| Last night, he went to the hotel. | 昨日の晩、ホテルに行きました。<br>**Kinō no ban, hoteru ni ikimashita.**<br>(kee-noh noh ban hoh-te-roo nee ik-ee-mash-ta) |

| | |
|---|---|
| Last night, he went to the hotel with me. | 昨日の晩、私とホテルに行きました。<br>**Kinō no ban, watashi to hoteru ni ikimashita.**<br>(kee-noh noh ban wa-tash to hoh-te-roo nee ik-ee-mash-ta) |
| 's | の<br>**no**<br>(noh) |
| reservation | 予約<br>**yoyaku**<br>(yoh-ya-koo) |
| a hotel reservation / the hotel reservation | ホテルの予約<br>**hoteru no yoyaku**<br>(hoh-te-roo noh yoh-ya-koo) |
| I made a hotel reservation. | ホテルの予約をしました。<br>**Hoteru no yoyaku o shimashita.**<br>(hoh-te-roo noh yoh-ya-koo o shee-mash-ta) |
| Did you make a hotel reservation? | ホテルの予約をしましたか。<br>**Hoteru no yoyaku o shimashita ka?**<br>(hoh-te-roo noh yoh-ya-koo o shee-mash-ta ka) |
| internet / the internet | インターネット<br>**intānetto**<br>(in-tah-ne-toh) |
| on the internet / online | インターネットで<br>**intānetto de**<br>(in-tah-ne-toh day) |
| I made a hotel reservation online. | インターネットでホテルの予約をしました。<br>**Intānetto de hoteru no yoyaku o shimashita.**<br>(in-tah-ne-toh day hoh-te-roo noh yoh-ya-koo o shee-mash-ta) |

| | |
|---|---|
| Last night, I made a hotel reservation online. | 昨日の晩、インターネットでホテルの予約をしました。<br>**Kinō no ban, intānetto de hoteru no yoyaku o shimashita.**<br>(kee-noh noh ban in-tah-ne-toh day hoh-te-roo noh yoh-ya-koo o shee-mash-ta) |
| I / he / she / they / we / you go / will go / are going to go | 行きます<br>**ikimasu**<br>(ik-ee-mass) |
| Kyoto | 京都<br>**Kyōto**<br>(kee-oh-toh) |
| I'm going to go to Kyoto. | 京都に行きます。<br>**Kyōto ni ikimasu.**<br>(kee-oh-toh nee ik-ee-mass) |
| Last night, I made a hotel reservation online – we're going to go to Kyoto! | 昨日の晩、インターネットでホテルの予約をしました。京都に行きます。<br>**Kinō no ban, intānetto de hoteru no yoyaku o shimashita – Kyōto ni ikimasu!**<br>(kee-noh noh ban in-tah-ne-toh day hoh-te-roo noh yoh-ya-koo o shee-mash-ta – kee-oh-toh nee ik-ee-mass) |
| Are you going to go to Kyoto? | 京都に行きますか。<br>**Kyōto ni ikimasu ka?**<br>(kee-oh-toh nee ik-ee-mass ka) |
| bus / the bus / a bus | バス<br>**basu**<br>(bus-oo) |
| by bus | バスで<br>**basu de**<br>(bus-oo day) |

| | |
|---|---|
| Are you going to go to Kyoto by bus? | バスで京都に行きますか。<br>**Basu de Kyōto ni ikimasu ka?**<br>(bus-oo day kee-oh-toh nee ik-ee-mass ka) |
| today | 今日<br>**kyō**<br>(kyoh) |
| I'm going to go to Kyoto by bus today. | 今日、バスで京都に行きます。<br>**Kyō, basu de Kyōto ni ikimasu.**<br>(kyoh bus-oo day kee-oh-toh nee ik-ee-mass) |
| taxi | タクシー<br>**takushii**<br>(tak-oo-shee) |
| by taxi | タクシーで<br>**takushii de**<br>(tak-oo-shee day) |
| Osaka | 大阪<br>**Ōsaka**<br>(oh-sah-ka) |
| Today, they're going to go to Osaka by taxi. | 今日、タクシーで大阪に行きます。<br>**Kyō, takushii de Ōsaka ni ikimasu.**<br>(kyoh tak-oo-shee day oh-sah-ka nee ik-ee-mass) |
| this afternoon | 今日の午後<br>**kyō no gogo**<br>(kyoh noh goh-goh) |
| This afternoon, are you going to go to Osaka by taxi? | 今日の午後、タクシーで大阪に行きますか。<br>**Kyō no gogo, takushii de Ōsaka ni ikimasu ka?**<br>(kyoh noh goh-goh tak-oo-shee day oh-sah-ka nee ik-ee-mass ka) |
| train | 電車<br>**densha**<br>(den-sha) |

| | |
|---|---|
| to Hiroshima | 広島に<br>**Hiroshima ni**<br>(hi-ro-shee-ma nee) |
| Are you going to go to Hiroshima by train? | 電車で広島に行きますか。<br>**Densha de Hiroshima ni ikimasu ka?**<br>(den-sha day day hi-ro-shee-ma nee ik-ee-mass ka) |
| Are you going to go to Hiroshima by train with Mrs Suzuki today? | 今日、鈴木さんと電車で広島に行きますか。<br>**Kyō, Suzuki san to densha de Hiroshima ni ikimasu ka?**<br>(kyoh su-zoo-kee sun to den-sha day day hi-ro-shee-ma nee ik-ee-mass ka) |
| family / the family / my family | 家族<br>**kazoku**<br>(ka-zok) |
| I'm going to go to Hiroshima by bus with my family this afternoon. | 今日の午後、家族とバスで広島に行きます。<br>**Kyō no gogo, kazoku to basu de Hiroshima ni ikimasu.**<br>(kyoh noh goh-goh ka-zok to bus-oo day hi-ro-shee-ma nee ik-ee-mass) |
| your family | ご家族<br>**go kazoku**<br>(goh ka-zok) |
| Are you going to go to the department store with your family by taxi today? | 今日、ご家族とタクシーでデパートに行きますか。<br>**Kyō, go kazoku to takushii de depāto ni ikimasu ka?**<br>(kyoh goh ka-zok to tak-oo-shee day day-par-toh nee ik-ee-mass ka) |
| beer / the beer | ビール<br>**biiru**<br>(bee-roo) |
| the hotel restaurant / the hotel's restaurant | ホテルのレストラン<br>**hoteru no resutoran**<br>(hoh-te-roo noh res-toh-run) |

|  |  |
|---|---|
| I drank beer in the hotel restaurant. | ホテルのレストランでビールを飲みました。<br>**Hoteru no resutoran de biiru o nomimashita.**<br>(hoh-te-roo noh res-toh-run day bee-roo o no-mee-mash-ta) |
| bar / the bar | バー<br>**bā**<br>(bar) |
| I drank beer in the bar. | バーでビールを飲みました。<br>**Bā de biiru o nomimashita.**<br>(bar day bee-roo o no-mee-mash-ta) |
| the hotel bar / the hotel's bar | ホテルのバー<br>**hoteru no bā**<br>(hoh-te-roo noh bar) |
| Did you drink beer in the hotel bar with Mr Tanaka today? | 今日、田中さんとホテルのバーでビールを飲みましたか。<br>**Kyō, Tanaka san to hoteru no bā de biiru o nomimashita ka?**<br>(kyoh ta-na-ka sun to hoh-te-roo no bar day bee-roo o no-mee-mash-ta ka) |
| park / the park | 公園<br>**kōen**<br>(ko-en) |
| football / soccer | サッカー<br>**sakkā**<br>(sa-kaa) |
| Are you going to play football in the park with your family this afternoon? | 今日の午後、ご家族と公園でサッカーをしますか。<br>**Kyō no gogo, go kazoku to kōen de sakkā o shimasu ka?**<br>(kyo noh goh-goh go ka-zok to ko-en day sa-kaa o shee-mass ka) |
| weather / the weather | 天気<br>**tenki**<br>(ten-kee) |

| | |
|---|---|
| Word that helps add some emphasis to the word that it goes after; it can also make it clear that this is the subject you're talking about and it's also often used when someone has just noticed something. | が<br>**ga**<br>(ga) |
| The weather is good. | 天気がいいです。<br>**Tenki ga ii desu.**<br>(ten-kee ga ee-ee dess) |
| so | から<br>**kara**<br>(ka-ra) |
| The weather is good so I'm going to play football in the park with my family. | 天気がいいですから、家族と公園でサッカーをします。<br>**Tenki ga ii desu kara kazoku to kōen de sakkā o shimasu.**<br>(ten-kee ga ee-ee dess, ka-ra ka-zok to ko-en day saa-ka o shee-mass) |
| I / he / she / we / they / you watched | 見ました<br>**mimashita**<br>(mee-mash-ta) |
| sumo | 相撲<br>**sumō**<br>(soo-moh) |
| on TV | テレビで<br>**terebi de**<br>(te-re-bee day) |
| this morning | 今朝<br>**kesa**<br>(ke-sa) |
| This morning, we watched sumo on TV. | 今朝、テレビで相撲を見ました。<br>**Kesa, terebi de sumō o mimashita.**<br>(ke-sa te-re-bee day soo-moh o mee-mash-ta) |
| anime | アニメ<br>**anime**<br>(a-nee-may) |

| | |
|---|---|
| **yesterday morning** | 昨日の朝<br>**kinō no asa**<br>(kee-noh noh a-sa) |
| **Yesterday morning, we watched an anime on TV.** | 昨日の朝、テレビでアニメを見ました。<br>**Kinō no asa, terebi de anime o mimashita.**<br>(kee-noh noh a-sa te-re-bee day a-nee-may o mee-mash-ta) |

Well, that's it, you're done with chapter four! Remember, don't try to hold onto or remember anything you've learnt here. Everything you learnt in earlier chapters will be brought back up and reinforced in later chapters. You don't need to do anything or make any effort to memorise anything.

## Forget what you were taught at school!

Many of us were told at school that we did not have an aptitude for languages, that we didn't have a "knack" or a "gift" for them.

Well, if this applies to you, then please let me assure you that this is all absolute nonsense! If you are able to read these words in front of you then this demonstrates that you've been able to learn English and, if you can learn one language, then your brain is just as capable of learning another – it simply needs to be approached in the right way!

In fact, since you've got as far as the end of Chapter Four, it should already be obvious to you that you are quite capable of learning a foreign language when it's taught in the right way. The secret to success for you will be choosing the right materials once you're finished with this book (more on that later).

# CHAPTER 5

Shall we watch an anime
on TV this evening?
Or shall we go out?

## Shall we watch an anime on TV this evening? Or shall we go out?

Personally, I'd watch the anime.

I mean, there's nothing I like more than watching an animated drama about a high school student who becomes a ghost slayer after he mysteriously develops supernatural powers following a freak accident involving a god of death, a bowl of ramen and the girl he's secretly in love with. I mean, who hasn't had that happen to them at least once in their lives?!

Anyway… whether the plots of animes are always entirely plausible or not, let's get back to building some sentences!

What is "we watched"?

見ました
**mimashita**
(mee-mash-ta)

And how would you say "we watched sumo"?

相撲を見ました。
**Sumō o mimashita.**
(soo-moh o mee-mash-ta)

What is "on TV"?

テレビで
**terebi de**
(te-re-bee day)

And so how would you say "we watched sumo on TV"?

テレビで相撲を見ました。
**Terebi de sumō o mimashita.**
(te-re-bee day soo-moh o mee-mash-ta)

How about "we watched sumo on TV last night"?

昨日の晩、テレビで相撲を見ました。
**Kinō no ban, terebi de sumō o mimashita.**
(kee-noh noh ban te-re-bee day soo-moh o mee-mash-ta)

What is "anime" or "the anime" or "an anime"?

アニメ
**anime**
(a-nee-may)

And what is "yesterday morning"?

昨日の朝
**kinō no asa**
(kee-noh noh a-sa)

And so how would you say "yesterday morning, we watched an anime on TV"?

昨日の朝、テレビでアニメを見ました。
**Kinō no asa, terebi de anime o mimashita.**
(kee-noh noh a-sa te-re-bee day a-nee-may o mee-mash-ta)

How about "yesterday morning, I watched an anime on TV"?

昨日の朝、テレビでアニメを見ました。
**Kinō no asa, terebi de anime o mimashita.**
(kee-noh noh a-sa te-re-bee day a-nee-may o mee-mash-ta)

And how would you say "Yesterday morning, *I* watched an anime on TV with my family"?

昨日の朝、家族とテレビでアニメを見ました。
**Kinō no asa, kazoku to terebi de anime o mimashita.**
(kee-noh noh a-sa ka-zok to te-re-bee day a-nee-may o mee-mash-ta)

How would you say "it was interesting"?

面白かったです。
**Omoshirokatta desu!**
(om-osh-ee-ro-ka-ta dess)

So now say "Yesterday morning, I watched an anime on TV with my family. It was interesting!":

昨日の朝、家族とテレビでアニメを見ました。面白かったです。

**Kinō no asa, kazoku to terebi de anime o mimashita. Omoshirokatta desu!**

(kee-noh noh a-sa ka-zok to te-re-bee day a-nee-may o mee-mash-ta. om-osh-ee-ro-ka-ta dess)

If "I watch" is "mimashita" how would you say "I watch" / "I will watch" / "I'm going to watch"?

見ます
**mimasu**
(mee-mass)

And what is "this morning"?

今朝
**kesa**
(ke-sa)

So how would you say "I'm going to watch an anime this morning"?

今朝、アニメを見ます。
**Kesa, anime o mimasu.**
(ke-sa a-nee-may o mee-mass)

What is "sumo"?

相撲
**sumō**
(soo-moh)

So how would you say "I'm going to watch sumo on TV with my family this morning"?

今朝、家族とテレビで相撲を見ます。
**Kesa, kazoku to terebi de sumō o mimasu.**
(ke-sa ka-zok to te-re-bee day soo-moh o mee-mass)

198

What is "yesterday morning"?

昨日の朝
**kinō no asa**
(kee-noh noh a-sa)

And what is "I watch", "I will watch", "I'm going to watch"?

見ます
**mimasu**
(mee-mass)

And what was "I watched"?

見ました
**mimashita**
(mee-mash-ta)

And what is "I go", "I will go", and "I'm going to go"?

行きます
**ikimasu**
(ik-ee-mass)

And what is "I went"?

行きました
**ikimashita**
(ik-ee-mash-ta)

And what is "I eat" / "I will eat" / "I'm going to eat"?

食べます
**tabemasu**
(tab-ay-mass)

And what is "I ate"?

食べました
**tabemashita**
(ta-bay-mash-ta)

What is "I drink" / "I will drink" / "I'm going to drink"?

飲みます
**nomimasu**
(no-mee-mass)

And what is "I drank"?

飲みました
**nomimashita**
(no-mee-mash-ta)

What is "I do" / "I play" / "I will do" / "I will play" / "I'm going to do" / "I'm going to play"?

します
**shimasu**
(shee-mass)

And what is "I did" / "I played"?

しました
**shimashita**
(shee-mash-ta)

So, we're very used to changing the ends of these words in Japanese, either to "mashita" if we want to talk about the past or to "masu" if we want to talk about the present or future.

I'm now going to teach you another way in which you can change the end of such words so that you can express even more ideas.

What we're going to do is, instead of ending these words with "mashita" or "masu", we are going to end them with "masho" – pronounced "ma-shore".

Let's do that now!

Take "I did" / "I played" – shimashita – and replace the "mashita" on the end with "masho" (ma-shore). Do that now, what do you get?

しましょう
**shimashō**
(shee-ma-shore)

And that means "*let's do*" or "*let's play*."

So how would you say "let's play basketball"?

バスケットボールをしましょう！
**Basuketobōru o shimashō!**
(bask-et-oh-bor-oo o shee-ma-shore)

And how would you say "let's play tennis"?

テニスをしましょう！
**Tenisu o shimashō!**
(te-ni-soo o shee-ma-shore)

What about "let's play football"?

サッカーをしましょう！
**Sakkā o shimashō!**
(sa-kaa o shee-ma-shore)

What is "I ate"?

食べました
**tabemashita**
(ta-bay-mash-ta)

And so how do you think you would say "let's eat"?

食べましょう！
**Tabemashō!**
(ta-bay-ma-shore)

How about "Let's eat katsu curry!"?

カツカレーを食べましょう！
**Katsu karē o tabemashō!**
(kats ka-ray o ta-bay-ma-shore)

And "let's eat miso ramen"?

みそラーメンを食べましょう！
**Miso rāmen o tabemashō!**
(mee-soh ra-men o ta-bay-ma-shore)

Tokyo

"This evening" or "tonight" in Japanese is:

今晩
**konban**
(kon-ban)

So how would you say "let's eat miso ramen tonight"?

今晩、みそラーメンを食べましょう！
**Konban, miso rāmen o tabemashō!**
(kon-ban mee-soh ra-men o ta-bay-ma-shore)

And how would you say "let's eat sushi tonight"?

今晩、すしを食べましょう！
**Konban, sushi o tabemashō!**
(kon-ban sushi o ta-bay-ma-shore)

What is "I went"?

行きました
**ikimashita**
(ik-ee-mash-ta)

And what is "I go" / "I will go" / "I'm going to go"?

行きます
**ikimasu**
(ik-ee-mass)

And so how would you say "Let's go"?

行きましょう！
**Ikimashō!**
(ik-ee-ma-shore)

How about "Let's go to a bar this evening"?

今晩、バーに行きましょう！
**Konban, bā ni ikimashō!**
(kon-ban bar nee ik-ee-ma-shore)

And what about "Let's go to Hokkaido this evening"?

今晩、北海道に行きましょう！
**Konban, Hokkaidō ni ikimashō!**
(kon-ban ho-kai-doh nee ik-ee-ma-shore)

What is "I drank"?

飲みました
**nomimashita**
(no-mee-mash-ta)

And so how would you say "let's drink"?

飲みましょう！
**Nomimashō!**
(no-mee-ma-shore)

And how would you say "Let's drink beer tonight"?

今晩、ビールを飲みましょう！
**Konban, biiru o nomimashō!**
(kon-ban bee-roo o no-mee-ma-shore)

How about "let's drink beer with Mr Suzuki tonight"?

今晩、鈴木さんとビールを飲みましょう！
**Konban, Suzuki san to biiru o nomimashō!**
(kon-ban su-zoo-kee sun to bee-roo o no-mee-ma-shore)

What is "I watched"?

見ました
**mimashita**
(mee-mash-ta)

And what is "I watch" / "I will watch" / "I'm going to watch"?

見ます
**mimasu**
(mee-mass)

And so how would you say "let's watch"?

見ましょう！
**Mimashō!**
(mee-ma-shore)

And "let's watch an anime tonight"?

今晩、アニメを見ましょう！
**Konban, anime o mimashō!**
(kon-ban a-nee-may o mee-ma-shore)

What is "on TV"?

テレビで
**terebi de**
(te-re-bee day)

So now say "Let's watch an anime on TV tonight".

今晩、テレビでアニメを見ましょう！
**Konban, terebi de anime o mimashō!**
(kon-ban te-re-bee day a-nee-may o mee-ma-shore)

"I went out" in Japanese is:

出かけました
**dekakemashita**
(day-ka-kay-mash-ta)

So how would you say "This morning, I went out"?

今朝、出かけました。
**Kesa, dekakemashita.**
(ke-sa day-ka-kay-mash-ta)

How about "This morning, I went out with my family"?

今朝、家族と出かけました。
**Kesa, kazoku to dekakemashita.**
(ke-sa ka-zok to day-ka-kay-mash-ta)

What is "your family"?

ご家族
**go kazoku**
(goh ka-zok)

So how would you say "you went out with your family this morning"?

今朝、ご家族と出かけました。
**Kesa, go kazoku to dekakemashita.**
(ke-sa goh ka-zok to day-ka-kay-mash-ta)

Turn that into a question and ask "did you go out with your family this morning?"

今朝、ご家族と出かけましたか。
**Kesa, go kazoku to dekakemashita ka?**
(ke-sa goh ka-zok to day-ka-kay-mash-ta ka)

Again, what is "yesterday morning"?

昨日の朝
**kinō no asa**
(kee-noh noh a-sa)

So how would you say "did you go out with your family yesterday morning?"

昨日の朝、ご家族と出かけましたか。
**Kinō no asa, go kazoku to dekakemashita ka?**
(kee-noh noh a-sa goh ka-zok to day-ka-kay-mash-ta ka)

If "I went out" is "dekakemashita," how do you think you would say "I go out" /
"I will go out" / "I'm going to go out"?

出かけます
**dekakemasu**
(day-ka-kay-mass)

And so how would you say "I'm going to go out tonight"?

今晩、出かけます。
**Konban, dekakemasu.**
(kon-ban day-ka-kay-mass)

What is "I drank"?

飲みました
**nomimashita**
(no-mee-mash-ta)

And what is "I drink"?

飲みます
**nomimasu**
(no-mee-mass)

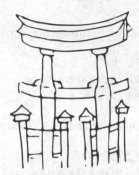

And what is "Let's drink"?

飲みましょう！
**Nomimashō!**
(no-mee-ma-shore)

And again, what is "I went out"?

出かけました
**dekakemashita**
(day-ka-kay-mash-ta)

And what is "I go out" / "I will go out" / "I'm going to go out"?

出かけます
**dekakemasu**
(day-ka-kay-mass)

And so how do you think you'd say "*let's* go out"?

出かけましょう
**Dekakemashō!**
(day-ka-kay-ma-shore)

And "let's go out today"?

今日、出かけましょう！
**Kyō, dekakemashō!**
(kyoh day-ka-kay-ma-shore)

How about "let's go out tonight"?

今晩、出かけましょう！
**Konban, dekakemashō!**
(kon-ban day-ka-kay-ma-shore)

And once again, what is "Let's drink beer"?

ビールを飲みましょう！
**Biiru o nomimashō!**
(bee-roo no-mee-ma-shore)

And what is "let's eat katsu curry"?

カツカレーを食べましょう！
**Katsu karē o tabemashō!**
(kats ka-ray o tab-ay-ma-shore)

And what is "let's go to Hokkaido"?

北海道に行きましょう！
**Hokkaidō ni ikimashō!**
(ho-kai-doh nee ik-ee-ma-shore)

And again, how would you say "let's go out tonight"?

今晩、出かけましょう！
**Konban, dekakemashō!**
(kon-ban day-ka-kay-ma-shore)

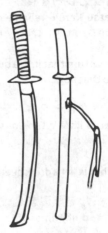

How would you say "Let's watch"?

見ましょう！
**Mimashō!**
(mee-ma-shore)

And how would you say "let's watch an anime tonight"?

今晩、アニメを見ましょう！
**Konban, anime o mimashō!**
(kon-ban a-nee-may o mee-ma-shore)

Now, one of the wonderful things about knowing how to say "let's" in Japanese is that it means you also know how to say "shall we…?" I'll show you what I mean:

What is "let's go to Hokkaido"?

北海道に行きましょう！
**Hokkaidō ni ikimashō!**
(ho-kai-doh nee ik-ee-ma-shore)

Now, I want you to add "ka" onto the end of that sentence. Do that now – say literally "let's go to Hokkaido ka?"

北海道に行きましょうか。
**Hokkaidō ni ikimashō ka?**
(ho-kai-doh nee ik-ee-ma-shore ka)

And that means "shall we go to Hokkaido?"

How would you say "let's eat katsu curry"?

カツカレーを食べましょう！
**Katsu karē o tabemashō!**
(kats ka-ray o tab-ay-ma-shore)

Now, turn that into a question and, by doing so, ask "shall we eat katsu curry?" Do that now:

カツカレーを食べましょうか。
**Katsu karē o tabemashō ka?**
(kats ka-ray o tab-ay-ma-shore ka)

What is "let's drink beer"?

ビールを飲みましょう！
**Biiru o nomimashō!**
(bee-roo o no-mee-ma-shore)

So how would you say "shall we drink beer?"

ビールを飲みましょうか。
**Biiru o nomimashō ka?**
(bee-roo o no-mee-ma-shore ka)

So, as you can see, when we add "masho" (ma-shore) onto the end of a word, it becomes "let's…" If we then also add a "ka" it becomes "shall we…?"

Let's try doing this once more. Again, what is "let's go out"?

出かけましょう！
**Dekakemashō!**
(day-ka-kay-ma-shore)

And what is "let's go out tonight"?

今晩、出かけましょう！
**Konban, dekakemashō!**
(kon-ban day-ka-kay-ma-shore)

Now, turn this into a question and ask "shall we go out tonight?"

今晩、出かけましょうか。
**Konban, dekakemashō ka?**
(kon-ban day-ka-kay-ma-shore ka)

"Or" in Japanese is:

それとも
**soretomo**
(so-re-to-moh)

So how would you say "…or shall we go out tonight?"

…それとも今晩、出かけましょうか。
**…soretomo konban, dekakemashō ka?**
(so ro to-mo kon-ban day-ka-kay ma shore ka)

What is "let's watch"?

見ましょう！
**Mimashō!**
(mee-ma-shore)

And "let's watch an anime"?

アニメを見ましょう！
**Anime o mimashō!**
(a-nee-may o mee-ma-shore)

**209**

And so how would you say "shall we watch an anime?"

アニメを見ましょうか。
**Anime o mimashō ka?**
(a-nee-may o mee-ma-shore ka)

What was "or"?

それとも
**soretomo**
(so-re-to-moh)

So how would you say "...or shall we watch an anime?"

…それともアニメを見ましょうか。
…**soretomo anime o mimashō ka?**
(so-re-to-mo a-nee-may o mee-ma-shore ka)

And how would you say "...or shall we watch an anime tonight?"

…それとも今晩、アニメを見ましょうか。
…**soretomo konban anime o mimashō ka?**
(so-re-to-mo kon-ban a-nee-may o mee-ma-shore ka)

Now again, how would you say "shall we go out?"

出かけましょうか。
**Dekakemashō ka?**
(day-ka-kay-ma-shore ka)

And how would you say "or shall we go out?"

…それとも出かけましょうか。
…**soretomo dekakemashō ka?**
(so-re-to-mo day-ka-kay-ma-shore ka)

And how would you say "shall we watch an anime on TV tonight?"

今晩、テレビでアニメを見ましょうか。
**Konban, terebi de anime o mimashō ka?**
(kon-ban te-re-bee day a-nee-may o mee-ma-shore ka)

Finally, how would you say "Shall we watch an anime on TV tonight? Or shall we go out?"

今晩、テレビでアニメを見ましょうか。それとも出かけましょうか。
**Konban, terebi de anime o mimashō ka? Soretomo dekakemashō ka?**
(kon-ban te-re-bee day a-nee-may o mee-ma-shore ka. so-re-to-mo day-ka-kay-ma-shore ka)

How did that go? There were some very complex aspects of Japanese you had to deal with in that sentence, so you should feel free to go over this chapter a number of times until you feel comfortable with everything it teaches you. Remember, this isn't a race; it's about going at your own pace and enjoying the learning experience. Take your time and only move on when you're ready.

Well, that's it! You've just finished your final chapter, which makes this your final checklist. Unlike the ones that came before it, however, you are not finished with this checklist until you can go the whole way through it without making a single mistake.

This doesn't mean that making mistakes when you go through it is a bad thing. It's just that I want you to return to it multiple times until going through the list becomes so easy that you can do so without making a single error.

When you can, it means you have really learnt what I wanted to teach you in these pages.

Now, get to it!

| | |
|---|---|
| 東京<br>**Tōkyō**<br>(toh-kee-oh) | Tokyo |
| に<br>**ni**<br>(nee) | to |
| 東京に<br>**Tōkyō ni**<br>(toh-kee-oh nee) | to Tokyo |
| 行きました<br>**ikimashita**<br>(ik-ee-mash-ta) | I went |
| レストラン<br>**resutoran**<br>(res-toh-run) | restaurant / the restaurant / a restaurant |
| レストランに行きました。<br>**Resutoran ni ikimashita.**<br>(res-toh-run nee ik-ee-mash-ta) | I went to the restaurant. |

| | |
|---|---|
| と<br>**to**<br>(to) | with |
| Paulと<br>**Paul to**<br>(paul to) | with Paul |
| Paulとレストランに行きました。<br>**Paul to resutoran ni ikimashita.**<br>(paul to res-toh-run nee ik-ee-mash-ta) | I went to the restaurant with Paul. |
| Paulと東京に行きました。<br>**Paul to Tōkyō ni ikimashita.**<br>(paul to toh-kee-oh nee ik-ee-mash-ta) | I went to Tokyo with Paul. |
| デパート<br>**depāto**<br>(day-par-toh) | department store / the department store / a department store |
| さん<br>**san**<br>(sun) | Mr / Mrs / Ms |
| 鈴木さん<br>**Suzuki san**<br>(su-zoo-kee sun) | Mr Suzuki / Mrs Suzuki / Ms Suzuki |
| 鈴木さんとデパートに行きました。<br>**Suzuki san to depāto ni ikimashita.**<br>(su-zoo-kee sun to day-par-toh nee ik-ee-mash-ta) | I went to the department store with Ms Suzuki. |
| 食べました<br>**tabemashita**<br>(ta-bay-mash-ta) | I ate |
| Paulと食べました。<br>**Paul to tabemashita.**<br>(paul to ta-bay-mash-ta) | I ate with Paul. |

| | |
|---|---|
| すし<br>**sushi**<br>(sushi) | sushi |
| を<br>**o**<br>(o) | *The word that you put after the thing that's been eaten.* |
| すしを食べました。<br>**Sushi o tabemashita.**<br>(sushi o ta-bay-mash-ta) | I ate sushi. |
| 鈴木さんとすしを食べました。<br>**Suzuki san to sushi o tabemashita.**<br>(su-zoo-kee sun to sushi o ta-bay-mash-ta) | I ate sushi with Mr Suzuki. |
| ラーメン<br>**rāmen**<br>(ra-men) | ramen / noodle soup |
| 鈴木さんとラーメンを食べました。<br>**Suzuki san to rāmen o tabemashita.**<br>(su-zoo-kee sun to ra-men o ta-bay-mash-ta) | I ate ramen with Mrs Suzuki. |
| で<br>**de**<br>(day) | in |
| レストランで<br>**resutoran de**<br>(res-toh-run day) | in the restaurant |
| 鈴木さんとレストランでラーメンを食べました。<br>**Suzuki san to resutoran de rāmen o tabemashita.**<br>(su-zoo-kee sun to res-toh-run day ra-men o ta-bay-mash-ta) | I ate ramen with Mrs Suzuki in the restaurant. |
| カツカレー<br>**katsu karē**<br>(kats ka-ray) | katsu curry |

| | |
|---|---|
| 田中さん<br>**Tanaka san**<br>(ta-na-ka sun) | Mr Tanaka / Mrs Tanaka / Ms Tanaka |
| 田中さんとレストランでカツカレーを食べました。<br>**Tanaka san to resutoran de katsu karē o tabemashita.**<br>(ta-na-ka sun to res-toh-run day kats ka-ray o ta-bay-mash-ta) | I ate katsu curry in the restaurant with Mr Tanaka. |
| デパートで<br>**depāto de**<br>(day-par-toh day) | in the department store |
| 田中さんとデパートでカツカレーを食べました。<br>**Tanaka san to depāto de katsu karē o tabemashita.**<br>(ta-na-ka sun to day-par-toh day kats ka-ray o ta-bay-mash-ta) | I ate katsu curry in the department store with Ms Tanaka. |
| あのデパート<br>**ano depāto**<br>(an-oh day-par-toh) | that department store |
| あのデパートで<br>**ano depāto de**<br>(an-oh day-par-toh day) | in that department store |
| 田中さんとあのデパートでカツカレーを食べました。<br>**Tanaka san to ano depāto de katsu karē o tabemashita.**<br>(ta-na-ka sun to an-oh day-par-toh day kats ka-ray o ta-bay-mash-ta) | I ate katsu curry in that department store with Ms Tanaka. |
| あのレストラン<br>**ano resutoran**<br>(an-oh res-toh-run) | that restaurant |
| あのレストランで<br>**ano resutoran de**<br>(an-oh res-toh-run day) | in that restaurant |

| | |
|---|---|
| 昨日<br>**kinō**<br>(kee-noh) | yesterday |
| 昨日、食べました<br>**kinō, tabemashita**<br>(kee-noh ta-bay-mash-ta) | yesterday, I ate |
| 昨日、鈴木さんとあのデパートでラーメンを食べました。<br>**Kinō, Suzuki san to ano resutoran de rāmen o tabemashita.**<br>(kee-noh su-zoo-kee sun to an-oh res-toh-run day ra-men o ta-bay-mash-ta) | Yesterday, I ate ramen in that restaurant with Mrs Suzuki. |
| 昨日の午後<br>**kinō no gogo**<br>(kee-noh noh goh-goh) | yesterday afternoon (literally "yesterday's afternoon") |
| 昨日の午後、鈴木さんと東京に行きました。<br>**Kinō no gogo, Suzuki san to Tōkyō ni ikimashita.**<br>(kee-noh noh goh-goh su-zoo-kee sun to toh-kee-oh nee ik-ee-mash-ta) | Yesterday afternoon, I went to Tokyo with Mrs Suzuki. |
| あのレストランに<br>**ano resutoran ni**<br>(an-oh res-toh-run nee) | to that restaurant |
| 昨日の晩<br>**kinō no ban**<br>(kee-noh noh ban) | yesterday evening / last night (literally "yesterday's evening") |
| 昨日の晩、田中さんとあのレストランに行きました。<br>**Kinō no ban, Tanaka san to ano resutoran ni ikimashita.**<br>(kee-noh noh ban ta-na-ka sun to res-toh-run nee ik-ee-mash-ta) | Yesterday evening, I went to that restaurant with Ms Tanaka. |
| 天ぷら<br>**tenpura**<br>(ten-poo-ra) | tempura |

| | |
|---|---|
| 食べました<br>**tabemashita**<br>(ta-bay-mash-ta) | she ate |
| 天ぷらを食べました。<br>**Tenpura o tabemashita.**<br>(ten-poo-ra o ta-bay-mash-ta) | She ate tempura. |
| レストランで天ぷらを食べました<br>**Resutoran de tenpura o tabemashita.**<br>(res-toh-run day ten-poo-ra o ta-bay-mash-ta) | She ate tempura in the restaurant. |
| あのレストランで天ぷらを食べました。<br>**Ano resutoran de tenpura o tabemashita.**<br>(an-oh res-toh-run day ten-poo-ra o ta-bay-mash-ta) | She ate tempura in that restaurant. |
| うどん<br>**udon**<br>(oo-don) | udon |
| 食べました<br>**tabemashita**<br>(ta-bay-mash-ta) | he ate |
| うどんを食べました。<br>**Udon o tabemashita.**<br>(oo-don o ta-bay-mash-ta) | He ate udon. |
| デパートでうどんを食べました。<br>**Depāto de udon o tabemashita.**<br>(day-par-toh day oo-don o ta-bay-mash-ta) | He ate udon in the department store. |
| あのデパートでうどんを食べました。<br>**Ano depāto de udon o tabemashita.**<br>(an-oh day-par-toh day oo-don o ta-bay-mash-ta) | He ate udon in that department store. |

| | |
|---|---|
| 昨日の午後、田中さんとあのデパートでうどんを食べました。<br>**Kinō no gogo, Tanaka san to ano depāto de udon o tabemashita.**<br>(kee-noh noh goh-goh ta-na-ka sun to an-oh day-par-toh day oo-don o ta-bay-mash-ta) | Yesterday afternoon, he ate udon in that department store with Mr Tanaka. |
| 食べました<br>**tabemashita**<br>(ta-bay-mash-ta) | we ate |
| うどんを食べました。<br>**Udon o tabemashita.**<br>(oo-don o ta-bay-mash-ta) | We ate udon. |
| 昨日の晩、うどんを食べました。<br>**Kinō no ban, udon o tabemashita.**<br>(kee-noh noh ban oo-don o ta-bay-mash-ta) | We ate udon last night. |
| 沖縄<br>**Okinawa**<br>(ok-ee-now-a) | Okinawa |
| 昨日の晩、沖縄でうどんを食べました。<br>**Kinō no ban, Okinawa de udon o tabemashita.**<br>(kee-noh noh ban ok-ee-now-a day oo-don o ta-bay-mash-ta) | We ate udon in Okinawa last night. |
| 行きました<br>**ikimashita**<br>(ik-ee-mash-ta) | she went |
| 行きました<br>**ikimashita**<br>(ik-ee-mash-ta) | he went |
| 行きました<br>**ikimashita**<br>(ik-ee-mash-ta) | we went |

| | |
|---|---|
| 昨日の午後、あのレストランに行きました。<br>**Kinō no gogo, ano resutoran ni ikimashita.**<br>(kee-noh noh goh-goh an-oh res-toh-run nee ik-ee-mash-ta) | We went to that restaurant yesterday afternoon. |
| 北海道<br>**Hokkaidō**<br>(ho-kai-doh) | Hokkaido |
| 昨日、北海道に行きました。<br>**Kinō, Hokkaidō ni ikimashita.**<br>(kee-noh ho-kai-doh nee ik-ee-mash-ta.) | We went to Hokkaido yesterday. |
| 札幌<br>**Sapporo**<br>(sa-po-roh) | Sapporo |
| 札幌で食べました。<br>**Sapporo de tabemashita.**<br>(sa-po-roh day ta-bay-mash-ta) | We ate in Sapporo. |
| みそラーメン<br>**miso rāmen**<br>(mee-soh ra-men) | miso ramen |
| 札幌でみそラーメンを食べました。<br>**Sapporo de miso rāmen o tabemashita.**<br>(sa-po-roh day mee-soh ra-men o ta-bay-mash-ta) | We ate miso ramen in Sapporo. |
| 昨日、北海道に行きました。札幌でみそラーメンを食べました。<br>**Kinō, Hokkaidō ni ikimashita. Sapporo de miso rāmen o tabemashita.**<br>(kee-noh ho-kai-doh nee ik-ee-mash-ta. sa-po-roh day mee-soh ra-men o ta-bay-mash-ta) | We went to Hokkaido yesterday.<br>We ate miso ramen in Sapporo. |

| | |
|---|---|
| です<br>**desu**<br>(dess) | it is |
| みそラーメンです。<br>**Miso rāmen desu.**<br>(mee-soh ra-men dess) | It's miso ramen. |
| デパートです。<br>**Depāto desu.**<br>(day-par-toh dess) | It's a department store. |
| おいしかった<br>**Oishikatta**<br>(oy-sh-ka-ta) | was delicious |
| おいしかったです！<br>**Oishikatta desu!**<br>(oy-sh-ka-ta dess) | It was delicious! |
| 昨日の午後、札幌でみそラーメンを食べました。おいしかったです！<br>**Kinō no gogo, Sapporo de miso rāmen o tabemashita. Oishikatta desu!**<br>(kee-noh noh goh-goh, sa-po-roh day mee-soh ra-men o ta-bay-mash-ta. oy-sh-ka-ta dess) | Yesterday afternoon, I ate miso ramen in Sapporo. It was delicious! |
| 昨日、北海道に行きました。札幌でみそラーメンを食べました。おいしかったです！<br>**Kinō, Hokkaido ni ikimashita. Sapporo de miso rāmen o tabemashita. Oishikatta desu!**<br>(kee-noh, ho-kai-doh nee ik-ee-mash-ta. sa-po-roh day mee-soh ra-men o ta-bay-mash-ta. oy-sh-ka-ta dess) | Yesterday, we went to Hokkaido. We ate miso ramen in Sapporo. It was delicious. |
| 行きました<br>**ikimashita**<br>(ik-ee-mash-ta) | they went |

| | |
|---|---|
| 京都に<br>**Kyōto ni**<br>(kee-oh-toh nee) | to Kyoto |
| 京都に行きました。<br>**Kyōto ni ikimashita.**<br>(kee-oh-toh nee ik-ee-mash-ta) | They went to Kyoto. |
| 私と<br>**watashi to**<br>(wa-ta-sh to) | with me |
| 私と京都に行きました。<br>**Watashi to Kyōto ni ikimashita.**<br>(wa-ta-sh to kee-oh-toh nee ik-ee-mash-ta) | They went to Kyoto with me. |
| 先週<br>**sen shū**<br>(sen shoo) | last week |
| 先週、私と京都に行きました。<br>**Sen shū, watashi to Kyōto ni ikimashita.**<br>(sen shoo, wa-ta-sh to kee-oh-toh nee ik-ee-mash-ta) | Last week, they went to Kyoto with me. |
| 面白かった<br>**omoshirokatta**<br>(om-osh-ee-ro-ka-ta) | was interesting |
| 面白かったです！<br>**Omoshirokatta desu!**<br>(om-osh-ee-ro-ka-ta dess) | It was interesting! |
| 先週、山中さんと京都に行きました。面白かったです。<br>**Sen shū, Tanaka san to Kyōto ni ikimashita. Omoshirokatta desu.**<br>(sen shoo, ta-na-ka sun to kee-oh-toh nee ik-ee-mash-ta. om-osh-ee-ro-ka-ta dess) | Last week, we went to Kyoto with Mrs Tanaka. It was interesting. |
| うつくしかった<br>**utsukushikatta**<br>(oo-tsoo-koo-shee-ka-ta) | was beautiful |

| | |
|---|---|
| 美しかったです！<br>**Utsukushikatta desu!**<br>(oo-tsoo-koo-shee-ka-ta dess) | It was beautiful! |
| 先週、田中さんと沖縄に行きました。美しかったです。<br>**Sen shū, Tanaka san to Okinawa ni ikimashita. Utsukushikatta desu!**<br>(sen shoo, ta-na-ka sun to ok-ee-now-a nee ik-ee-mash-ta. oo-tsoo-koo-shee-ka-ta dess) | Last week, we went to Okinawa with Mrs Tanaka. It was beautiful. |
| しました<br>**shimashita**<br>(shee-mash-ta) | I / he / she / they / we / you did<br>I / he / she / they / we / you played |
| バスケットボール<br>**basuketobōru**<br>(bask-et-oh-bor-oo) | basketball |
| バスケットボールをしました。<br>**Basuketobōru o shimashita.**<br>(bask-et-oh-bor-oo o shee-mash-ta) | We played basketball. |
| 昨日、札幌でバスケットボールをしました。<br>**Kinō, Sapporo de basuketobōru o shimashita.**<br>(kee-noh sa-po-roh day bask-et-oh-bor-oo o shee-mash-ta) | Yesterday, we played basketball in Sapporo. |
| か<br>**ka**<br>(ka) | spoken question mark |
| 先週、バスケットボールをしましたか。<br>**Sen shū, basuketobōru o shimashita ka?**<br>(sen shoo bask-et-oh-bor-oo o shee-mash-ta ka) | Did you play basketball last week? |
| テニス<br>**tenisu**<br>(ten-ee-soo o) | tennis |

| | |
|---|---|
| 先週、テニスをしましたか。<br>**Sen shū, tenisu o shimashita ka?**<br>(sen shoo ten-ee-soo o shee-mash-ta ka) | Did you play tennis last week? |
| 先週、鈴木さんとテニスをしましたか。<br>**Sen shū Suzuki san to tenisu o shimashita ka?**<br>(sen shoo su-zoo-kee sun to ten-ee-soo o shee-mash-ta ka) | Last week, did you play tennis with Mr Suzuki? |
| ホテル<br>**hoteru**<br>(hoh-te-roo) | hotel / the hotel / a hotel |
| 昨日の晩、ホテルに行きました。<br>**Kinō no ban, hoteru ni ikimashita.**<br>(kee-noh noh ban hoh-te-roo nee ik-ee-mash-ta) | Last night, he went to the hotel. |
| 昨日の晩、私とホテルに行きました。<br>**Kinō no ban, watashi to hoteru ni ikimashita.**<br>(kee-noh noh ban wa-tash to hoh-te-roo nee ik-ee-mash-ta) | Last night, he went to the hotel with me. |
| の<br>**no**<br>(noh) | 's |
| 予約<br>**yoyaku**<br>(yoh-ya-koo) | reservation |
| ホテルの予約<br>**hoteru no yoyaku**<br>(hoh-te-roo noh yoh-ya-koo) | a hotel reservation / the hotel reservation |
| ホテルの予約をしました。<br>**Hoteru no yoyaku o shimashita.**<br>(hoh-te-roo noh yoh-ya-koo o shee-mash-ta) | I made a hotel reservation. |

| | |
|---|---|
| ホテルの予約をしましたか。<br>**Hoteru no yoyaku o shimashita ka?**<br>(hoh-te-roo noh yoh-ya-koo o shee-mash-ta ka) | Did you make a hotel reservation? |
| インターネット<br>**intānetto**<br>(in-tah-ne-toh) | internet / the internet |
| インターネットで<br>**intānetto de**<br>(in-tah-ne-toh day) | on the internet / online |
| インターネットでホテルの予約をしました。<br>**Intānetto de hoteru no yoyaku o shimashita.**<br>(in-tah-ne-toh day hoh-te-roo noh yoh-ya-koo o shee-mash-ta) | I made a hotel reservation online. |
| 昨日の晩、インターネットでホテルの予約をしました。<br>**Kinō no ban, intānetto de hoteru no yoyaku o shimashita.**<br>(kee-noh noh ban in-tah-ne-toh day hoh-te-roo noh yoh-ya-koo o shee-mash-ta) | Last night, I made a hotel reservation online. |
| 行きます<br>**ikimasu**<br>(ik-ee-mass) | I / he / she / they / we / you go / will go / are going to go |
| 京都<br>**Kyōto**<br>(kee-oh-toh) | Kyoto |
| 京都に行きます。<br>**Kyōto ni ikimasu.**<br>(kee-oh-toh nee ik-ee-mass) | I'm going to go to Kyoto. |

| | |
|---|---|
| 昨日の晩、インターネットでホテルの予約をしました。京都に行きます。<br>**Kinō no ban, intānetto de hoteru no yoyaku o shimashita – Kyōto ni ikimasu!**<br>(kee-noh noh ban in-tah-ne-toh day hoh-te-roo noh yoh-ya-koo o shee-mash-ta – kee-oh-toh nee ik-ee-mass) | Last night, I made a hotel reservation online – we're going to go to Kyoto! |
| 京都に行きますか。<br>**Kyōto ni ikimasu ka?**<br>(kee-oh-toh nee ik-ee-mass ka) | Are you going to go to Kyoto? |
| バス<br>**basu**<br>(bus-oo) | bus / the bus / a bus |
| バスで<br>**basu de**<br>(bus-oo day) | by bus |
| バスで京都に行きますか。<br>**Basu de Kyōto ni ikimasu ka?**<br>(bus-oo day kee-oh-toh nee ik-ee-mass ka) | Are you going to go to Kyoto by bus? |
| 今日<br>**kyō**<br>(kyoh) | today |
| 今日、バスで京都に行きます。<br>**Kyō, basu de Kyōto ni ikimasu.**<br>(kyoh bus-oo day kee-oh-toh nee ik-ee-mass) | I'm going to go to Kyoto by bus today. |
| タクシー<br>**takushii**<br>(tak-oo-shee) | taxi |
| タクシーで<br>**takushii de**<br>(tak-oo-shee day) | by taxi |

| | |
|---|---|
| 大阪<br>**Ōsaka**<br>(oh-sah-ka) | Osaka |
| 今日、タクシーで大阪に行きます。<br>**Kyō, takushii de Ōsaka ni ikimasu.**<br>(kyoh tak-oo-shee day oh-sah-ka nee ik-ee-mass) | Today, they're going to go to Osaka by taxi. |
| 今日の午後<br>**kyō no gogo**<br>(kyoh noh goh-goh) | this afternoon |
| 今日の午後、タクシーで大阪に行きますか。<br>**Kyō no gogo, takushii de Ōsaka ni ikimasu ka?**<br>(kyoh noh goh-goh tak-oo-shee day oh-sah-ka nee ik-ee-mass ka) | This afternoon, are you going to go to Osaka by taxi? |
| 電車<br>**densha**<br>(den-sha) | train |
| 広島に<br>**Hiroshima ni**<br>(hi-ro-shee-ma nee) | to Hiroshima |
| 電車で広島に行きますか。<br>**Densha de Hiroshima ni ikimasu ka?**<br>(den-sha day day hi-ro-shee-ma nee ik-ee-mass ka) | Are you going to go to Hiroshima by train? |
| 今日、鈴木さんと電車で広島に行きますか。<br>**Kyō, Suzuki san to densha de Hiroshima ni ikimasu ka?**<br>(kyoh su-zoo-kee sun to den-sha day day hi-ro-shee-ma nee ik-ee-mass ka) | Are you going to go to Hiroshima by train with Mrs Suzuki today? |
| 家族<br>**kazoku**<br>(ka-zok) | family / the family / my family |

| | |
|---|---|
| 今日の午後、家族とバスで広島に行きます。<br>**Kyō no gogo, kazoku to basu de Hiroshima ni ikimasu.**<br>(kyoh noh goh-goh ka-zok to bus-oo day hi-ro-shee-ma nee ik-ee-mass) | I'm going to go to Hiroshima by bus with my family this afternoon. |
| ご家族<br>**go kazoku**<br>(goh ka-zok) | your family |
| 今日、ご家族とタクシーでデパートに行きますか。<br>**Kyō, go kazoku to takushii de depāto ni ikimasu ka?**<br>(kyoh goh ka-zok to tak-oo-shee day day-par-toh nee ik-ee-mass ka) | Are you going to go to the department store with your family by taxi today? |
| ビール<br>**biiru**<br>(bee-roo) | beer / the beer |
| ホテルのレストラン<br>**hoteru no resutoran**<br>(hoh-te-roo noh res-toh-run) | the hotel restaurant / the hotel's restaurant |
| ホテルのレストランでビールを飲みました。<br>**Hoteru no resutoran de biiru o nomimashita.**<br>(hoh-te-roo noh res-toh-run day bee-roo o no-mee-mash-ta) | I drank beer in the hotel restaurant. |
| バー<br>**bā**<br>(bar) | bar / the bar |
| バーでビールを飲みました。<br>**Bā de biiru o nomimashita.**<br>(bar day bee-roo o no-mee-mash-ta) | I drank beer in the bar. |
| ホテルのバー<br>**hoteru no bā**<br>(hoh-te-roo noh bar) | the hotel bar / the hotel's bar |

| | |
|---|---|
| 今日、田中さんとホテルのバーでビールを飲みましたか。<br>**Kyō, Tanaka san to hoteru no bā de biiru o nomimashita ka?**<br>(kyoh ta-na-ka sun to hoh-te-roo no bar day bee-roo o no-mee-mash-ta ka) | Did you drink beer in the hotel bar with Mr Tanaka today? |
| 公園<br>**kōen**<br>(ko-en) | park / the park |
| サッカー<br>**sakkā**<br>(sa-kaa) | football / soccer |
| 今日の午後、ご家族と公園でサッカーをしますか。<br>**Kyō no gogo, go kazoku to kōen de sakkā o shimasu ka?**<br>(kyo noh goh-goh go ka-zok to ko-en day sa-kaa o shee-mass ka) | Are you going to play football in the park with your family this afternoon? |
| 天気<br>**tenki**<br>(ten-kee) | weather / the weather |
| 今日の天気<br>**Kyō no tenki**<br>(kyoh noh ten-kee) | today's weather |
| 天気がいいです。<br>**Tenki ga ii desu.**<br>(kyoh noh ten-kee ee-ee dess) | Today's weather is good. |
| から<br>**kara**<br>(ka-ra) | so |
| 天気がいいですから、家族と公園でサッカーをします。<br>**Tenki ga ii desu kara kazoku to kōen de sakkā o shimasu.**<br>(kyoh noh ten-kee ee-ee dess, ka-ra ka-zok to ko-en day aa-ka o shee-mass) | Today's weather is good so I'm going to play football in the park with my family. |

| | |
|---|---|
| 見ました<br>**mimashita**<br>(mee-mash-ta) | I / he / she / we / they / you watched |
| 相撲<br>**sumō**<br>(soo-moh) | sumo |
| テレビ<br>**terebi de**<br>(te-re-bee day) | on TV |
| 今朝<br>**kesa**<br>(ke-sa) | this morning |
| 今朝、テレビで相撲を見ました。<br>**Kesa, terebi de sumō o mimashita.**<br>(ke-sa te-re-bee day soo-moh o mee-mash-ta) | This morning, we watched sumo on TV. |
| アニメ<br>**anime**<br>(a-nee-may) | anime |
| 昨日の朝<br>**kinō no asa**<br>(kee-noh noh a-sa) | yesterday morning |
| 昨日の朝、テレビでアニメを見ました。<br>**Kinō no asa, terebi de anime o mimashita.**<br>(kee-noh noh a-sa te-re-bee day a-nee-may o mee-mash-ta) | Yesterday morning, we watched an anime on TV. |
| しましょう!<br>**Shimashō!**<br>(shee-ma-shore) | Let's play…! / Let's do…! |
| バスケットボールをしましょう!<br>**Basuketobōru o shimashō!**<br>(bask-et-oh-bor-oo o shee-ma-shore) | Let's play basketball! |

| | |
|---|---|
| 食べましょう！<br>**Tabemashō!**<br>(ta-bay-ma-shore) | Let's eat! |
| 今晩<br>**konban**<br>(kon-ban) | this evening / tonight |
| 今晩、みそラーメンを食べましょう！<br>**Konban, miso rāmen o tabemashō!**<br>(kon-ban mee-soh ra-men o ta-bay-ma-shore) | This evening, let's eat miso ramen! |
| 行きましょう！<br>**Ikimashō!**<br>(ik-ee-ma-shore) | Let's go! |
| 今晩、バーに行きましょう！<br>**Konban, bā ni ikimashō!**<br>(kon-ban bar nee ik-ee-ma-shore) | Let's go to a bar tonight! |
| 飲みましょう！<br>**Nomimashō!**<br>(no-mee-ma-shore) | Let's drink! |
| 今晩、鈴木さんとビールを飲みましょう！<br>**Konban, Suzuki san to biiru o nomimashō!**<br>(kon-ban su-zoo-kee sun to bee-roo o no-mee-ma-shore) | Let's drink beer with Mrs Suzuki tonight! |
| 見ましょう！<br>**Mimashō!**<br>(mee-ma-shore) | Let's watch! |
| 今晩、テレビでアニメを見ましょう！<br>**Konban, terebi de anime o mimashō!**<br>(kon-ban te-re-bee day a-nee-may o mee-ma-shore) | Let's watch an anime on TV this evening! |

| | |
|---|---|
| 出かけました<br>**dekakemashita**<br>(day-ka-kay-mash-ta) | I / he / she / we / they / you went out |
| 昨日の朝、ご家族と出かけましたか。<br>**Kinō no asa, go kazoku to dekakemashita ka?**<br>(kee-noh noh a-sa goh ka-zok to day-ka-kay-mash-ta ka) | Yesterday morning, did you go out with your family? |
| 出かけます<br>**dekakemasu**<br>(day-ka-kay-mass) | I / he / she / we / they / you go out / will go out / are going to go out |
| 今晩、出かけます。<br>**Konban, dekakemasu.**<br>(kon-ban day-ka-kay-mass) | I'm going to go out this evening. |
| 出かけましょう！<br>**Dekakemashō!**<br>(day-ka-kay-ma-shore) | Let's go out! |
| 今晩、出かけましょう！<br>**Konban, dekakemashō!**<br>(kon-ban day-ka-kay-ma-shore) | Let's go out this evening! |
| 行きましょうか。<br>**Ikimashō ka?**<br>(ik-ee-ma-shore ka) | Shall we go? |
| 北海道に行きましょうか。<br>**Hokkaidō ni ikimashō ka?**<br>(ho-kai-doh nee ik-ee-ma-shore ka) | Shall we go to Hokkaido? |
| 食べましょうか。<br>**Tabemashō ka?**<br>(tab-ay-ma-shore ka) | Shall we eat? |
| カツカレーを食べましょうか。<br>**Katsu karē o tabemashō ka?**<br>(kats ka-ray o tab-ay-ma-shore ka) | Shall we eat katsu curry? |
| 飲みましょうか。<br>**Nomimashō ka?**<br>(no-mee-ma-shore ka) | Shall we drink? |

| | |
|---|---|
| ビールを飲みましょうか。<br>**Biiru o nomimashō ka?**<br>(bee-roo o no-mee-ma-shore ka) | Shall we drink beer? |
| 出かけましょうか。<br>**Dekakemashō ka?**<br>(day-ka-kay-ma-shore ka) | Shall we go out? |
| 今晩、出かけましょうか。<br>**Konban, dekakemashō ka?**<br>(kon-ban day-ka-kay-ma-shore ka) | Shall we go out this evening? |
| それとも<br>**soretomo**<br>(so-re-to-moh) | or |
| 今晩、テレビでアニメを見ましょうか。それとも出かけましょうか。<br>**Konban, terebi de anime o mimashō ka? Soretomo dekakemashō ka?**<br>(kon-ban te-re-bee day a-nee-may o mee-ma-shore ka. so-re-to-mo day-ka-kay-ma-shore ka) | Shall we watch an anime on TV this evening? Or shall we go out? |

Having worked your way through the Japanese-to-English list above without making any mistakes, you will now want to get to the point where you can also work through the English-to-Japanese list below without making any mistakes. You should feel free to do this over multiples days or even weeks if you feel you need to. Just take your time and work at it until constructing the sentences and recalling the words become second nature to you.

| | |
|---|---|
| Tokyo | 東京<br>**Tōkyō**<br>(toh-kee-oh) |
| to | に<br>**ni**<br>(nee) |

| | |
|---|---|
| to Tokyo | 東京に<br>**Tōkyō ni**<br>(toh-kee-oh nee) |
| I went | 行きました<br>**ikimashita**<br>(ik-ee-mash-ta) |
| restaurant / the restaurant /<br>a restaurant | レストラン<br>**resutoran**<br>(res-toh-run) |
| I went to the restaurant. | レストランに行きました。<br>**Resutoran ni ikimashita.**<br>(res-toh-run nee ik-ee-mash-ta) |
| with | と<br>**to**<br>(to) |
| with Paul | Paulと<br>**Paul to**<br>(paul to) |
| I went to the restaurant with Paul. | Paulとレストランに行きました。<br>**Paul to resutoran ni ikimashita.**<br>(paul to res-toh-run nee ik-ee-<br>mash-ta) |
| I went to Tokyo with Paul. | Paulと東京に行きました。<br>**Paul to Tōkyō ni ikimashita.**<br>(paul to toh-kee-oh nee ik-ee-<br>mash-ta) |
| department store / the<br>department store / a department<br>store | デパート<br>**depato**<br>(day-par-toh) |
| Mr / Mrs / Ms | さん<br>**san**<br>(sun) |
| Mr Suzuki / Mrs Suzuki / Ms Suzuki | 鈴木さん<br>**Suzuki san**<br>(su-zoo-kee sun) |

| | |
|---|---|
| I went to the department store with Ms Suzuki. | 鈴木さんとデパートに行きました。<br>**Suzuki san to depāto ni ikimashita.**<br>(su-zoo-kee sun to day-par-toh nee ik-ee-mash-ta) |
| I ate | 食べました<br>**tabemashita**<br>(ta-bay-mash-ta) |
| I ate with Paul. | Paulと食べました。<br>**Paul to tabemashita.**<br>(paul to ta-bay-mash-ta) |
| sushi | すし<br>**sushi**<br>(sushi) |
| *The word that you put after the thing that's been eaten.* | を<br>**o**<br>(o) |
| I ate sushi. | すしを食べました。<br>**Sushi o tabemashita.**<br>(sushi o ta-bay-mash-ta) |
| I ate sushi with Mr Suzuki. | 鈴木さんとすしを食べました。<br>**Suzuki san to sushi o tabemashita.**<br>(su-zoo-kee sun to sushi o ta-bay-mash-ta) |
| ramen / noodle soup | ラーメン<br>**rāmen**<br>(ra-men) |
| I ate ramen with Mrs Suzuki. | 鈴木さんとラーメンを食べました。<br>**Suzuki san to rāmen o tabemashita.**<br>(su-zoo-kee sun to ra-men o ta-bay-mash-ta) |
| in | で<br>**de**<br>(day) |

| | |
|---|---|
| in the restaurant | レストランで<br>**resutoran de**<br>(res-toh-run day) |
| I ate ramen with Mrs Suzuki in the restaurant. | 鈴木さんとレストランでラーメンを食べました。<br>**Suzuki san to resutoran de rāmen o tabemashita.**<br>(su-zoo-kee sun to res-toh-run day ra-men o ta-bay-mash-ta) |
| katsu curry | カツカレー<br>**katsu karē**<br>(kats ka-ray) |
| Mr Tanaka / Mrs Tanaka / Ms Tanaka | 田中さん<br>**Tanaka san**<br>(ta-na-ka sun) |
| I ate katsu curry in the restaurant with Mr Tanaka. | 田中さんとレストランでカツカレーを食べました。<br>**Tanaka san to resutoran de katsu karē o tabemashita.**<br>(ta-na-ka sun to res-toh-run day kats ka-ray o ta-bay-mash-ta) |
| in the department store | デパートで<br>**depāto de**<br>(day-par-toh day) |
| I ate katsu curry in the department store with Ms Tanaka. | 田中さんとデパートでカツカレーを食べました。<br>**Tanaka san to depāto de katsu karē o tabemashita.**<br>(ta-na-ka sun to day-par-toh day kats ka-ray o ta-bay-mash-ta) |
| that department store | あのデパート<br>**ano depāto**<br>(an-oh day-par-toh) |
| in that department store | あのデパートで<br>**ano depāto de**<br>(an-oh day-par-toh day) |

| | |
|---|---|
| I ate katsu curry in that department store with Ms Tanaka. | 田中さんとあのデパートでカツカレーを食べました。<br>**Tanaka san to ano depāto de katsu karē o tabemashita.**<br>(ta-na-ka sun to an-oh day-par-toh day kats ka-ray o ta-bay-mash-ta) |
| that restaurant | あのレストラン<br>**ano resutoran**<br>(an-oh res-toh-run) |
| in that restaurant | あのレストランで<br>**ano resutoran de**<br>(an-oh res-toh-run day) |
| yesterday | 昨日<br>**kinō**<br>(kee-noh) |
| yesterday, I ate | 昨日、食べました<br>**kinō, tabemashita**<br>(kee-noh ta-bay-mash-ta) |
| Yesterday, I ate ramen in that restaurant with Mrs Suzuki. | 昨日、鈴木さんとあのレストランでラーメンを食べました。<br>**Kinō, Suzuki san to ano resutoran de rāmen o tabemashita.**<br>(kee-noh su-zoo-kee sun to an-oh res-toh-run day ra-men o ta-bay-mash-ta) |
| yesterday afternoon (literally "yesterday's afternoon") | 昨日の午後<br>**kinō no gogo**<br>(kee-noh noh goh-goh) |
| Yesterday afternoon, I went to Tokyo with Mrs Suzuki. | 昨日の午後、鈴木さんと東京に行きました。<br>**Kinō no gogo, Suzuki san to Tōkyō ni ikimashita.**<br>(kee-noh noh goh-goh su-zoo-kee sun to toh-kee-oh nee ik-ee-mash-ta) |
| to that restaurant | あのレストランに<br>**ano resutoran ni**<br>(an-oh res-toh-run nee) |

| | |
|---|---|
| yesterday evening / last night (literally "yesterday's evening") | 昨日の晩<br>**kinō no ban**<br>(kee-noh noh ban) |
| Yesterday evening, I went to that restaurant with Ms Tanaka. | 昨日の晩、田中さんとあのレストランに行きました。<br>**Kinō no ban, Tanaka san to ano resutoran ni ikimashita.**<br>(kee-noh noh ban ta-na-ka sun to res-toh-run nee ik-ee-mash-ta) |
| tempura | 天ぷら<br>**tenpura**<br>(ten-poo-ra) |
| she ate | 食べました<br>**tabemashita**<br>(ta-bay-mash-ta) |
| She ate tempura. | 天ぷらを食べました。<br>**Tenpura o tabemashita.**<br>(ten-poo-ra o ta-bay-mash-ta) |
| She ate tempura in the restaurant. | レストランで天ぷらを食べました。<br>**Resutoran de tenpura o tabemashita.**<br>(res-toh-run day ten-poo-ra o ta-bay-mash-ta) |
| She ate tempura in that restaurant. | あのレストランで天ぷらを食べました。<br>**Ano resutoran de tenpura o tabemashita.**<br>(ah-oh res-toh-run day ten-poo-ra o ta-bay-mash-ta) |
| udon | うどん<br>**udon**<br>(oo-don) |
| he ate | 食べました<br>**tabemashita**<br>(ta-bay-mash-ta) |

| | |
|---|---|
| He ate udon. | うどんを食べました。<br>**Udon o tabemashita.**<br>(*oo-don o ta-bay-mash-ta*) |
| He ate udon in the department store. | デパートでうどんを食べました。<br>**Depāto de udon o tabemashita.**<br>(*day-par-toh day oo-don o ta-bay-mash-ta*) |
| He ate udon in that department store. | あのデパートでうどんを食べました。<br>**Ano depāto de udon o tabemashita.**<br>(*an-oh day-par-toh day oo-don o ta-bay-mash-ta*) |
| Yesterday afternoon, he ate udon in that department store with Mr Tanaka. | 昨日の午後、田中さんとあのデパートでうどんを食べました。<br>**Kinō no gogo, Tanaka san to ano depāto de udon o tabemashita.**<br>(*kee-noh noh goh-goh ta-na-ka sun to an-oh day-par-toh day oo-don o ta-bay-mash-ta*) |
| we ate | 食べました<br>**tabemashita**<br>(*ta-bay-mash-ta*) |
| We ate udon. | うどんを食べました。<br>**Udon o tabemashita.**<br>(*oo-don o ta-bay-mash-ta*) |
| We ate udon last night. | 昨日の晩、うどんを食べました。<br>**Kinō no ban, udon o tabemashita.**<br>(*kee-noh noh ban oo-don o ta-bay-mash-ta*) |
| Okinawa | 沖縄<br>**Okinawa**<br>(*ok-ee-now-a*) |
| We ate udon in Okinawa last night. | 昨日の晩、沖縄でうどんを食べました。<br>**Kinō no ban, Okinawa de udon o tabemashita.**<br>(*kee-noh noh ban ok-ee-now-a day oo-don o ta-bay-mash-ta*) |

| | |
|---|---|
| she went | 行きました<br>**ikimashita**<br>(ik-ee-mash-ta) |
| he went | 行きました<br>**ikimashita**<br>(ik-ee-mash-ta) |
| we went | 行きました<br>**ikimashita**<br>(ik-ee-mash-ta) |
| We went to that restaurant yesterday afternoon. | 昨日の午後、あのレストランに行きました。<br>**Kinō no gogo, ano resutoran ni ikimashita.**<br>(kee-noh noh goh-goh an-oh res-toh-run nee ik-ee-mash-ta) |
| Hokkaido | 北海道<br>**Hokkaidō**<br>(ho-kai-doh) |
| We went to Hokkaido yesterday. | 昨日、北海道に行きました。<br>**Kinō, Hokkaidō ni ikimashita.**<br>(kee-noh ho-kai-doh nee ik-ee-mash-ta.) |
| Sapporo | 札幌<br>**Sapporo**<br>(sa-po-roh) |
| We ate in Sapporo. | 札幌で食べました。<br>**Sapporo de tabemashita.**<br>(sa-po-roh day ta-bay-mash-ta) |
| miso ramen | みそラーメン<br>**miso rāmen**<br>(mee-soh ra-men) |
| We ate miso ramen in Sapporo. | 札幌でみそラーメンを食べました。<br>**Sapporo de miso rāmen o tabemashita.**<br>(sa-po-roh day mee-soh ra-men o ta-bay-mash-ta) |

| | |
|---|---|
| We went to Hokkaido yesterday. We ate miso ramen in Sapporo. | 昨日、北海道に行きました。札幌でみそラーメンを食べました。<br>**Kinō, Hokkaidō ni ikimashita. Sapporo de miso rāmen o tabemashita.**<br>(kee-noh ho-kai-doh nee ik-ee-mash-ta. sa-po-roh day mee-soh ra-men o ta-bay-mash-ta) |
| it is | です<br>**desu**<br>(dess) |
| It's miso ramen. | みそラーメンです。<br>**Miso rāmen desu.**<br>(mee-soh ra-men dess) |
| It's a department store. | デパートです。<br>**Depāto desu.**<br>(day-par-toh dess) |
| was delicious | おいしかった<br>**Oishikatta**<br>(oy-sh-ka-ta) |
| It was delicious! | おいしかったです！<br>**Oishikatta desu!**<br>(oy-sh-ka-ta dess) |
| Yesterday afternoon, I ate miso ramen in Sapporo. It was delicious! | 昨日の午後、札幌でみそラーメンを食べました。おいしかったです。<br>**Kinō no gogo, Sapporo de miso rāmen o tabemashita. Oishikatta desu!**<br>(kee-noh noh goh-goh, sa-po-roh day mee-soh ra-men o ta-bay-mash-ta. oy-sh-ka-ta dess) |

| | |
|---|---|
| Yesterday, we went to Hokkaido. We ate miso ramen in Sapporo. It was delicious. | 昨日、北海道に行きました。 札幌でみそラーメンを食べました。おいしかったです。<br>**Kinō, Hokkaidō ni ikimashita. Sapporo de miso rāmen o tabemashita. Oishikatta desu!**<br>(kee-noh, ho-kai-doh nee ik-ee-mash-ta. sa-po-roh day mee-soh ra-men o ta-bay-mash-ta. oy-sh-ka-ta dess) |
| they went | 行きました<br>**ikimashita**<br>(ik-ee-mash-ta) |
| to Kyoto | 京都に<br>**Kyōto ni**<br>(kee-oh-toh nee) |
| They went to Kyoto. | 京都に行きました。<br>**Kyōto ni ikimashita.**<br>(kee-oh-toh nee ik-ee-mash-ta) |
| with me | 私と<br>**watashi to**<br>(wa-ta-sh to) |
| They went to Kyoto with me. | 私と京都に行きました。<br>**Watashi to Kyōto ni ikimashita.**<br>(wa-ta-sh to kee-oh-toh nee ik-ee-mash-ta) |
| last week | 先週<br>**sen shū**<br>(sen shoo) |
| Last week, they went to Kyoto with me. | 先週、私と京都に行きました。<br>**Sen shū, watashi to Kyōto ni ikimashita.**<br>(sen shoo, wa-ta-sh to kee-oh-toh nee ik-ee-mash-ta) |
| was interesting | 面白かった<br>**omoshirokatta**<br>(om-osh-ee-ro-ka-ta) |

| | |
|---|---|
| It was interesting! | 面白かったです！<br>**Omoshirokatta desu!**<br>(om-osh-ee-ro-ka-ta dess) |
| Last week, we went to Kyoto with Mrs Tanaka. It was interesting. | 先週、田中さんと京都に行きました。面白かったです！<br>**Sen shū, Tanaka san to Kyōto ni ikimashita. Omoshirokatta desu!**<br>(sen shoo, ta-na-ka sun to kee-oh-toh nee ik-ee-mash-ta. om-osh-ee-ro-ka-ta dess) |
| was beautiful | 美しかった<br>**utsukushikatta**<br>(oo-tsoo-koo-shee-ka-ta) |
| It was beautiful! | 美しかったです！<br>**Utsukushikatta desu!**<br>(oo-tsoo-koo-shee-ka-ta dess) |
| Last week, we went to Okinawa with Mrs Tanaka. It was beautiful. | 先週、田中さんと沖縄に行きました。美しかったです！<br>**Sen shū, Tanaka san to Okinawa ni ikimashita. Utsukushikatta desu!**<br>(sen shoo, ta-na-ka sun to ok-ee-now-a nee ik-ee-mash-ta. oo-tsoo-koo-shee-ka-ta dess) |
| I / he / she / they / we / you did<br>I / he / she / they / we / you played | しました<br>**shimashita**<br>(shee-mash-ta) |
| basketball | バスケットボール<br>**basuketobōru**<br>(bask-et-oh-bor-oo) |
| We played basketball. | バスケットボールをしました。<br>**Basuketobōru o shimashita.**<br>(bask-et-oh-bor-oo o shee-mash-ta) |
| Yesterday, we played basketball in Sapporo. | 昨日、札幌でバスケットボールをしました。<br>**Kinō, Sapporo de basuketobōru o shimashita.**<br>(kee-noh sa-po-roh day bask-et-oh-bor-oo o shee-mash-ta) |

| | |
|---|---|
| *spoken question mark* | か<br>**ka**<br>(ka) |
| Did you play basketball last week? | 先週、バスケットボールをしましたか。<br>**Sen shū, basuketobōru o shimashita ka?**<br>(sen shoo bask-et-oh-bor-oo o shee-mash-ta ka) |
| tennis | テニス<br>**tenisu**<br>(ten-ee-soo o) |
| Did you play tennis last week? | 先週、テニスをしましたか。<br>**Sen shū, tenisu o shimashita ka?**<br>(sen shoo ten-ee-soo o shee-mash-ta ka) |
| Last week, did you play tennis with Mr Suzuki? | 先週、鈴木さんとテニスをしましたか。<br>**Sen shū, Suzuki san to tenisu o shimashita ka?**<br>(sen shoo su-zoo-kee sun to ten-ee-soo o shee-mash-ta ka) |
| hotel / the hotel / a hotel | ホテル<br>**hoteru**<br>(hoh-te-roo) |
| Last night, he went to the hotel. | 昨日の晩、ホテルに行きました。<br>**Kinō no ban, hoteru ni ikimashita.**<br>(kee-noh noh ban hoh-te-roo nee ik-ee mash ta) |
| Last night, he went to the hotel with me. | 昨日の晩、私とホテルに行きました。<br>**Kinō no ban, watashi to hoteru ni ikimashita.**<br>(kee-noh noh ban wa-tash to hoh-te-roo nee ik-ee-mash-ta) |
| 's | の<br>**no**<br>(noh) |

| | |
|---|---|
| reservation | 予約<br>**yoyaku**<br>(yoh-ya-koo) |
| a hotel reservation / the hotel reservation | ホテルの予約<br>**hoteru no yoyaku**<br>(hoh-te-roo noh yoh-ya-koo) |
| I made a hotel reservation. | ホテルの予約をしました。<br>**Hoteru no yoyaku o shimashita.**<br>(hoh-te-roo noh yoh-ya-koo o shee-mash-ta) |
| Did you make a hotel reservation? | ホテルの予約をしましたか。<br>**Hoteru no yoyaku o shimashita ka?**<br>(hoh-te-roo noh yoh-ya-koo o shee-mash-ta ka) |
| internet / the internet | インターネット<br>**intānetto**<br>(in-tah-ne-toh) |
| on the internet / online | インターネットで<br>**intānetto de**<br>(in-tah-ne-toh day) |
| I made a hotel reservation online. | インターネットでホテルの予約をしました。<br>**Intānetto de hoteru no yoyaku o shimashita.**<br>(in-tah-ne-toh day hoh-te-roo noh yoh-ya-koo o shee-mash-ta) |
| Last night, I made a hotel reservation online. | 昨日の晩、インターネットでホテルの予約をしました。<br>**Kinō no ban, intānetto de hoteru no yoyaku o shimashita.**<br>(kee-noh noh ban in-tah-ne-toh day hoh-te-roo noh yoh-ya-koo o shee-mash-ta) |
| I / he / she / they / we / you go / will go / are going to go | 行きます<br>**ikimasu**<br>(ik-ee-mass) |

| | |
|---|---|
| Kyoto | 京都<br>**Kyōto**<br>(kee-oh-toh) |
| I'm going to go to Kyoto. | 京都に行きます。<br>**Kyōto ni ikimasu.**<br>(kee-oh-toh nee ik-ee-mass) |
| Last night, I made a hotel reservation online – we're going to go to Kyoto! | 昨日の晩、インターネットでホテルの予約をしました。京都に行きます。<br>**Kinō no ban, intānetto de hoteru no yoyaku o shimashita – Kyōto ni ikimasu!**<br>(kee-noh noh ban in-tah-ne-toh day hoh-te-roo noh yoh-ya-koo o shee-mash-ta – kee-oh-toh nee ik-ee-mass) |
| Are you going to go to Kyoto? | 京都に行きますか。<br>**Kyōto ni ikimasu ka?**<br>(kee-oh-toh nee ik-ee-mass ka) |
| bus / the bus / a bus | バス<br>**basu**<br>(bus-oo) |
| by bus | バスで<br>**basu de**<br>(bus-oo day) |
| Are you going to go to Kyoto by bus? | バスで京都に行きますか。<br>**Basu de Kyōto ni ikimasu ka?**<br>(bus-oo day kee-oh-toh nec ik-ee-mass ka) |
| today | 今日<br>**kyō**<br>(kyoh) |
| I'm going to go to Kyoto by bus today. | 今日、バスで京都に行きます。<br>**Kyō, basu de Kyōto ni ikimasu.**<br>(kyoh bus-oo day kee-oh-toh nee ik-ee-mass) |

| | |
|---|---|
| taxi | タクシー<br>**takushii**<br>(tak-oo-shee) |
| by taxi | タクシーで<br>**takushii de**<br>(tak-oo-shee day) |
| Osaka | 大阪<br>**Ōsaka**<br>(oh-sah-ka) |
| Today, they're going to go to Osaka by taxi. | 今日、タクシーで大阪に行きます。<br>**Kyō, takushii de Ōsaka ni ikimasu.**<br>(kyoh tak-oo-shee day oh-sah-ka nee ik-ee-mass) |
| this afternoon | 今日の午後<br>**kyō no gogo**<br>(kyoh noh goh-goh) |
| This afternoon, are you going to go to Osaka by taxi? | 今日の午後、タクシーで大阪に行きますか。<br>**Kyō no gogo, takushii de Ōsaka ni ikimasu ka?**<br>(kyoh noh goh-goh tak-oo-shee day oh-sah-ka nee ik-ee-mass ka) |
| train | 電車<br>**densha**<br>(den-sha) |
| to Hiroshima | 広島に<br>**Hiroshima ni**<br>(hi-ro-shee-ma nee) |
| Are you going to go to Hiroshima by train? | 電車で広島に行きますか。<br>**Densha de Hiroshima ni ikimasu ka?**<br>(den-sha day day hi-ro-shee-ma nee ik-ee-mass ka) |

| | |
|---|---|
| Are you going to go to Hiroshima by train with Mrs Suzuki today? | 今日、鈴木さんと電車で広島に行きますか。<br>**Kyō, Suzuki san to densha de Hiroshima ni ikimasu ka?**<br>(kyoh su-zoo-kee sun to den-sha day day hi-ro-shee-ma nee ik-ee-mass ka) |
| family / the family / my family | 家族<br>**kazoku**<br>(ka-zok) |
| I'm going to go to Hiroshima by bus with my family this afternoon. | 今日の午後、家族とバスで広島に行きます。<br>**Kyō no gogo, kazoku to basu de Hiroshima ni ikimasu.**<br>(kyoh noh goh-goh ka-zok to bus-oo day hi-ro-shee-ma nee ik-ee-mass) |
| your family | ご家族<br>**go kazoku**<br>(goh ka-zok) |
| Are you going to go to the department store with your family by taxi today? | 今日、ご家族とタクシーでデパートに行きますか。<br>**Kyō, go kazoku to takushii de depāto ni ikimasu ka?**<br>(kyoh goh ka-zok to tak-oo-shee day day-par-toh nee ik-ee-mass ka) |
| beer / the beer | ビール<br>**biiru**<br>(bee-roo) |
| the hotel restaurant / the hotel's restaurant | ホテルのレストラン<br>**hoteru no resutoran**<br>(hoh-te-roo noh res-toh-run) |
| I drank beer in the hotel restaurant. | ホテルのレストランでビールを飲みました。<br>**Hoteru no resutoran de biiru o nomimashita.**<br>(hoh-te-roo noh res-toh-run day bee-roo o no-mee-mash-ta) |

| | |
|---|---|
| bar / the bar | バー<br>**bā**<br>(bar) |
| I drank beer in the bar. | バーでビールを飲みました。<br>**Bā de biiru o nomimashita.**<br>(bar day bee-roo o no-mee-mash-ta) |
| the hotel bar / the hotel's bar | ホテルのバー<br>**hoteru no bā**<br>(hoh-te-roo noh bar) |
| Did you drink beer in the hotel bar with Mr Tanaka today? | 今日、田中さんとホテルのバーでビールを飲みましたか。<br>**Kyō, Tanaka san to hoteru no bā de biiru o nomimashita ka?**<br>(kyoh ta-na-ka sun to hoh-te-roo no bar day bee-roo o no-mee-mash-ta ka) |
| park / the park | 公園<br>**kōen**<br>(ko-en) |
| football / soccer | サッカー<br>**sakkā**<br>(sa-kaa) |
| Are you going to play football in the park with your family this afternoon? | 今日の午後、ご家族と公園でサッカーをしますか。<br>**Kyō no gogo, go kazoku to kōen de sakkā o shimasu ka?**<br>(kyo noh goh-goh go ka-zok to ko-en day sa-kaa o shee-mass ka) |
| weather / the weather | 天気<br>**tenki**<br>(ten-kee) |
| today's weather | 今日の天気<br>**Kyō no tenki**<br>(kyoh noh ten-kee) |
| Today's weather is good. | 天気がいいです。<br>**Tenki ga ii desu.**<br>(ten-kee ga ee-ee dess) |

| | |
|---|---|
| so | から<br>**kara**<br>(ka-ra) |
| Today's weather is good so I'm going to play football in the park with my family. | 天気がいいですから、家族と公園でサッカーをします。<br>**Tenki ga ii desu kara kazoku to kōen de sakkā o shimasu.**<br>(ten-kee ga ee-ee dess, ka-ra ka-zok to ko-en day aa-ka o shee-mass) |
| I / he / she / we / they / you watched | 見ました<br>**mimashita**<br>(mee-mash-ta) |
| sumo | 相撲<br>**sumō**<br>(soo-moh) |
| on TV | テレビで<br>**terebi de**<br>(te-re-bee day) |
| this morning | 今朝<br>**kesa**<br>(ke-sa) |
| This morning, we watched sumo on TV. | 今朝、テレビで相撲を見ました。<br>**Kesa, terebi de sumō o mimashita.**<br>(ke-sa te-re-bee day soo-moh o mee-mash-ta) |
| anime | アニメ<br>**anime**<br>(a-nee-may) |
| yesterday morning | 昨日の朝<br>**kinō no asa**<br>(kee-noh noh a-sa) |
| Yesterday morning, we watched an anime on TV. | 昨日の朝、テレビでアニメを見ました。<br>**Kinō no asa, terebi de anime o mimashita.**<br>(kee-noh noh a-sa te-re-bee day a-nee-may o mee-mash-ta) |

| | |
|---|---|
| Let's play...! / Let's do...! | しましょう!<br>**Shimashō!**<br>(shee-ma-shore) |
| Let's play basketball! | バスケットボールをしましょう。<br>**Basuketobōru o shimashō!**<br>(bask-et-oh-bor-oo o shee-ma-shore) |
| Let's eat! | 食べましょう!<br>**Tabemashō!**<br>(ta-bay-ma-shore) |
| this evening / tonight | 今晩<br>**konban**<br>(kon-ban) |
| This evening, let's eat miso ramen! | 今晩、みそラーメンを食べましょう!<br>**Konban, miso rāmen o tabemashō!**<br>(kon-ban mee-soh ra-men o ta-bay-ma-shore) |
| Let's go! | 行きましょう!<br>**Ikimasho!**<br>(ik-ee-ma-shore) |
| Let's go to a bar tonight! | 今晩、バーに行きましょう!<br>**Konban, bā ni ikimashō!**<br>(kon-ban bar nee ik-ee-ma-shore) |
| Let's drink! | 飲みましょう!<br>**Nomimashō!**<br>(no-mee-ma-shore) |
| Let's drink beer with Mrs Suzuki tonight! | 今晩、鈴木さんとビールを飲みましょう!<br>**Konban, Suzuki san to biiru o nomimashō!**<br>(kon-ban su-zoo-kee sun to bee-roo o no-mee-ma-shore) |
| Let's watch! | 見ましょう!<br>**Mimashō!**<br>(mee-ma-shore) |

| | |
|---|---|
| Let's watch an anime on TV this evening! | 今晩、テレビでアニメを見ましょう！<br>**Konban, terebi de anime o mimashō!**<br>(kon-ban te-re-bee day a-nee-may o mee-ma-shore) |
| I / he / she / we / they / you went out | 出かけました<br>**dekakemashita**<br>(day-ka-kay-mash-ta) |
| Yesterday morning, did you go out with your family? | 昨日の朝、ご家族と出かけましたか。<br>**Kinō no asa, go kazoku to dekakemashita ka?**<br>(kee-noh noh a-sa goh ka-zok to day-ka-kay-mash-ta ka) |
| I / he / she / we / they / you go out / will go out / are going to go out | 出かけます<br>**dekakemasu**<br>(day-ka-kay-mass) |
| I'm going to go out this evening. | 今晩、出かけます。<br>**Konban, dekakemasu.**<br>(kon-ban day-ka-kay-mass) |
| Let's go out! | 出かけましょう！<br>**Dekakemashō!**<br>(day-ka-kay-ma-shore) |
| Let's go out this evening! | 今晩、出かけましょう！<br>**Konban, dekakemashō!**<br>(kon-ban day-ka-kay-ma-shore) |
| Shall we go? | 行きましょうか.<br>**Ikimashō ka?**<br>(ik-ee-ma-shore ka) |
| Shall we go to Hokkaido? | 北海道に行きましょうか。<br>**Hokkaidō ni ikimashō ka?**<br>(ho-kai-doh nee ik-ee-ma-shore ka) |
| Shall we eat? | 食べましょうか。<br>**Tabemashō ka?**<br>(tab-ay-ma-shore ka) |

| | |
|---|---|
| Shall we eat katsu curry? | カツカレーを食べましょうか。<br>**Katsu karē o tabemashō ka?**<br>(kats ka-ray o tab-ay-ma-shore ka) |
| Shall we drink? | 飲みましょうか。<br>**Nomimashō ka?**<br>(no-mee-ma-shore ka) |
| Shall we drink beer? | ビールを飲みましょうか。<br>**Biiru o nomimashō ka?**<br>(bee-roo o no-mee-ma-shore ka) |
| Shall we go out? | 出かけましょうか。<br>**Dekakemashō ka?**<br>(day-ka-kay-ma-shore ka) |
| Shall we go out this evening? | 今晩、出かけましょうか。<br>**Konban, dekakemashō ka?**<br>(kon-ban day-ka-kay-ma-shore ka) |
| or | それとも<br>**soretomo**<br>(so-re-to-moh) |
| Shall we watch an anime on TV this evening? Or shall we go out? | 今晩、テレビでアニメを見ましょうか。それとも出かけましょうか。<br>**Konban, terebi de anime o mimashō ka? Soretomo dekakemashō ka?**<br>(kon-ban te-re-bee day a-nee-may o mee-ma-shore ka. so-re-to-mo day-ka-kay-ma-shore ka) |

If you've got through this without making any mistakes then you're ready to read the final, but nevertheless essential, page of the book, which tells you what to do next.

well done for getting this far! well done indeed...

# What should I do next?

Well, here you are at the end of the final chapter. You have worked hard and yet a different journey now lies ahead of you!

The question you should be asking, of course, is: "what is that journey exactly?", "where do I go from here?" – essentially, "what should I do next?"

## well...

Well, that will depend to some degree on what you already knew when you began working through this book.

If you *have* found this book useful then I would recommend moving on to the audio course that I have produced entitled "Learn Japanese with Paul Noble". It uses the same method as this book except that you listen to it rather than read it. It will further develop your understanding of how to structure Japanese sentences while at the same time gently expanding your vocabulary in the language as well as teaching you plenty of tricks that will allow you to make rapid progress.

## And after that?

After that, I recommend that you find yourself a Japanese language exchange partner. This you will discover is very easy to do. Japanese speakers all around the world want a chance to practise their English, which means that you have something valuable to trade! Personally, I recommend chatting regularly either in person or online for twenty minutes in English followed by twenty minutes in Japanese.

Try to set a topic that you're going to discuss so that you can look up any relevant vocabulary in advance. Keep those words handy and then try to use them in conversation. If any of them are poorly translated or badly pronounced by you, you will quickly find out.

Make an effort to meet with the same speaker regularly and to return to old topics every couple of months. This will allow you to go back over old vocabulary and will also show you that you are in fact making progress, which will help keep you motivated.

If you follow this piece of advice, as well as the one above it, both you and your Japanese should soar!

Good Luck!